Trapping is my Life

Stoddart

Trapping is my Life

John Tetso

illustrated by
Lorne H. Bouchard, R.C.A.

Published in 1994 by
Stoddart Publishing Co. Limited
34 Lesmill Road
Toronto, Canada
M3B 2T6
(416) 445-3333

ISBN 0-7737-5705-8

PRINTING HISTORY
First published in hardcover
by Peter Martin Associates Limited in 1970
Second printing: 1976
Paperbound edition: 1977

Printed and bound in Canada

Contents

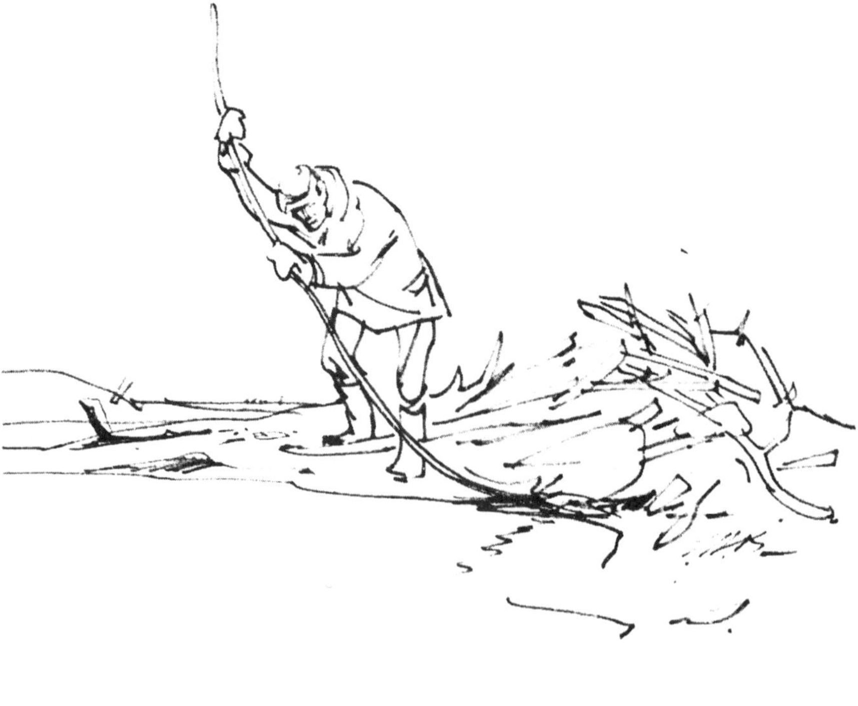

Preface

Our trip down the Mackenzie River in August, 1962 was inspired by Hugh MacLennan's book *Seven Rivers of Canada*. Everything he said of this great river was true, but to feel it one must travel it. We chartered a sixty-foot flat-bottomed boat, the *Liard River*, and set out from Hay River on August the eighth.

After running all day, each night we beached the boat, and it was on August 12 that we ran the boat in at Tsetso's* encampment. There was much excitement on board, this being our first true encounter with the people of the land. We scrambled ashore and naively invaded the privacy of the Tsetso's evening meal. The camp consisted of a tent, two clay-chinked log cabins, and the ever-present dogs.

The Tsetso family are of the Slavey tribe and Willow Lake River is their summer ground. John, his wife Jane, their children Virginia, Ernest, Florence, and Jane's father greeted us warmly

*Mrs. Molson uses the spelling of the name Tsetso which appears on government maps and surveys. In everyday practice, John's spelling, Tetso, is used as often.

but shyly. We joined them at their fire and talked of many things. We were most interested in their ways and life, also their language and ideas. John, who spoke English, told of his life. He had been elected chief of the Slaveys, but he found the demands on his time excessive, so he resigned although during his tenure as chief he met Prince Philip. He spoke of his life of trapping, of writing his stories, and of his woodwork: snowshoes, toboggans, even violins. He was a talented and resourceful man, who never ceased to inquire.

John was unlike any other Indian we met on the trip, quiet, thoughtful, sincere, and a conscientious family man. Industry was another of his qualities and it saddened him to see his friends leave the bush for the so-called ease of town life. He had a cabin at Fort Simpson, but he used it only at Christmas and as a supply depot. His children went to school, and he himself taught Ernest a good deal of wood lore, which stood the boy in good stead after his father's death.

Before we left Willow Lake River, John agreed to make three pair of snowshoes for our children, and that started our correspondence. We wrote to each other until his death and we exchanged gifts. He sent us skins: marten, beaver, cross fox, while we sent tea, cigarettes, clothes and coloured pencils for the girls. It was a happy and rewarding relationship for both sides. Each letter from John took us back to the North that we had come to love, and each letter from us showed that white people can be sincerely interested in their Indian brothers.

His untimely and unfortunate death from pneumonia left a great void for all who knew him and for his family. No one can put it into words. Ernest left school and became the head of the family, earning his living trapping, travelling the Tsetso lines as his father had taught him, in the unremitting cold of the northern winter. Virginia and Florence had problems adjusting and were cared for and watched over by Father Posset, who was a friend of John's. Walter, a newly adopted son, stayed with Jane, who remained with her father at Willow Lake River. The tragedy of John's death was that had he been in town or had he not lent his boat, he probably could have received medicinal treatment for his pneumonia, but his independence and the total lack of communications took his life.

Our common bond was broken, but Father Posset kept in touch by mail, and the publication of John's writings became a necessity, not only for the family's welfare, but that his efforts should not die with him and be lost.

John's stories may seem simple and short, but it is important to remember that they are all true and they took place in that part of Canada where the climate is unmerciful in winter, plagued by insects in summer, and the terrain is rugged. It is a land that does not permit mistakes, for mistakes more often than not lead to death.

Many thanks go to all John Tsetso's friends for their interest, but especially to those who persisted in the publication of this book: Father Posset, Fort Simpson; Bud Orange, MP for the Northwest Territories; Peter and Carol Martin, the publishers; and a special thanks to Lorne Bouchard RCA for his time and thought and talent, which he donated to illustrate so vividly moments in the stories.

Claire V. Molson
June 10, 1969

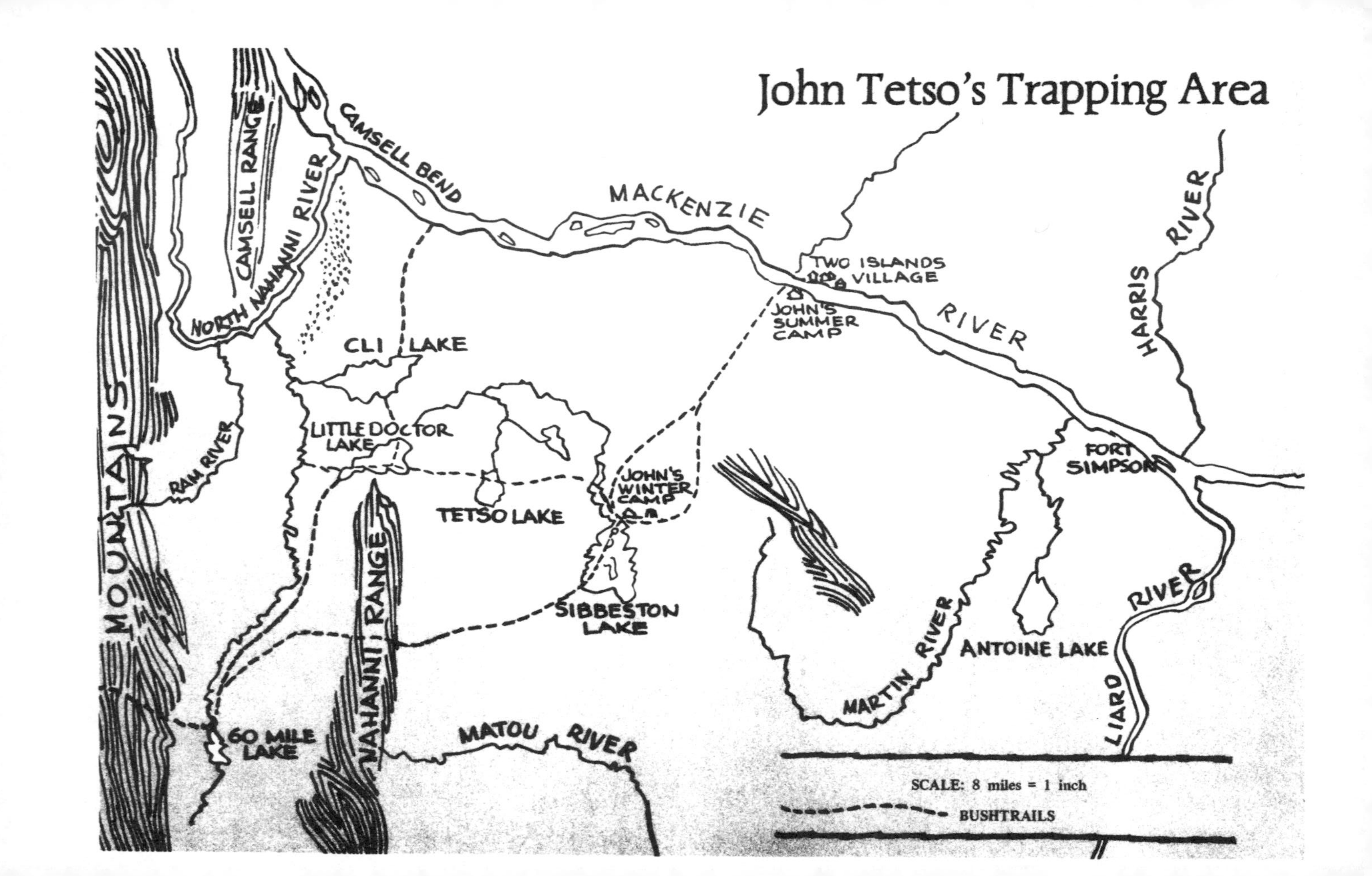
John Tetso's Trapping Area
CAMSELL RANGE
NORTH NAHANNI RIVER
CAMSELL BEND
MACKENZIE
RIVER
TWO ISLANDS VILLAGE
JOHN'S SUMMER CAMP
HARRIS RIVER
CLI LAKE
LITTLE DOCTOR LAKE
RAM RIVER
MOUNTAINS
TETSO LAKE
JOHN'S WINTER CAMP
SIBBESTON LAKE
FORT SIMPSON
NAHANNI RANGE
MARTIN RIVER
ANTOINE LAKE
LIARD RIVER
60 MILE LAKE
MATOU RIVER
SCALE: 8 miles = 1 inch
BUSHTRAILS

1 Spring Beaver Hunt

It has been suggested to me to write about life on the trapline. I am following that suggestion because I am always willing to help bridge the gap between our two worlds. Integration, that is.

First, I want to tell you a story of one little trip I made on my spring hunt. Later on, I will take you to the mountains, but if you have what they call acrophobia, the fear of high places, you cannot come with me. But I am sure you will not leave your chair just to read it, so I will do that too.

Yes, it was spring that day and summer laziness was already getting into my bones, but the beaver and muskrat season was still on, so I had work to do. I had brought my canoe to a creek on the south side of the lake by dog team before, so this time I went by land, on foot.

I had packed everything required for this trip into a packsack, so I took it down to the lake where a canoe was tied to the shore and got someone to paddle me across and return with the canoe. My little son wanted to go along, so I took him with me. First

day out we had to walk, and as snow was melting, we ran into water. Water, water everywhere, some places it was too deep for the younger man, so I stuck him on the top of my load, told him to hang on, and away I went. By evening, we had not reached our canoe, but found a beaver lodge and that was what we walked this far for.

Finding a dry spot, we built our camp, made a fire and started to cook a meal of fish. After we finished our supper of fish and bannock, I told Ernest that I was going to the beaver house, told him not to leave the camp and to watch the fire. I took a box of .22 long rifle shells and the rifle and started out in the direction of my beaver lodge. I did not go very far and water again. I sneaked up close to the lodge all right, but I had to stand in water till I got one, which took about two hours to show up. He did not come from the lodge itself; he came down along the shore and I got him before he reached the lodge. I got a pole long enough to reach him and I floated him in towards me and shore. I tied a length of string I had to one of his forward legs and started back to camp, me walking in water and pulling, the beaver floating and following behind.

I wanted to stay and maybe get another beaver, but I was a bit worried about my son. He was only five years old, and this was his first picnic. The lake ice had floated away above its winter bed and there was water many feet deep along the shore, which was only about eight feet from camp. He might try and make a bridge across this water and fall in. Besides that, I wanted to see how he was taking it. So, approaching camp, I walked slowly and sneaked. I did not see him right away, but after a while, a little head stuck out from behind one of the trees and bang, bang . . .

I asked him what he was doing. "Playing cowboy with the trees; that one is a bad cowboy, this one too, but that one is a good cowboy."

I started to skin my beaver, which does not take me long to do. Some white trappers say a beaver takes them half an hour to skin, others say it can't be done that quick; many a time I have skinned them in eight minutes flat, but I got to have good light and a good sharp knife for that.

That night, all the waterfowl seemed to be converging to this lake, Sibbeston Lake. All the time, we heard ducks, some flying overhead, others landing or taking off, and once in a while we heard splashes of water too. Fish could come close to shore, and ducks feeding on surface come on top of them, or sometimes a duck would touch a fish with his feet, and the fish take off for deeper water and the duck quack taking off too. His tone would show he was scared and that would make me laugh, wondering who scares who.

Early next day, I went to the beaver lodge, I caught one more beaver from this lodge in a trap I had set last night. I packed up after skinning the beaver, and we started for the creek and our canoe. Getting there, I opened a can of paint, put a light coat of paint on the canoe and waited two hours till the paint dried and hardened. Then I put it in the water, paddled up the creek, where we picked up some rocks to use as weights and went back down the river, setting a trap here and there.

At the mouth, we had dinner after setting a dozen traps. From here, all that afternoon, I paddled along the shore, seeing all kinds of ducks, including the loon and his necklace. By evening, we were way out on the south side of the lake, where we camped. I got eight beavers that day. They all went fine, except one: he sunk. Now some experts in the Game Department say that when a beaver is shot and sunk, that beaver is considered a loss. I am an expert too, but when that beaver sank, I did not consider it a loss at all.

I cut two poles long enough to reach the bottom, stuck one pole into the bottom at the spot where I saw air bubbles come up, and with the other pole I poked the bottom, feeling for the beaver. I did not work too hard before I touched him with my pole. So I stuck this pole into the bottom right beside him. Then I got the other pole, took my knife, split one end, took a box of matches out of my pocket, took one match and put it in the split to give so much a gap. With this pole, I went for him and when I felt him, I gave the pole a firm push. I knew that some of his long hair would get in that gap I made, so I started to turn the pole round and round in my hands, and sure enough, I began to feel some resistance at the other end of the pole. So I pulled and up came my beaver.

Next day, we went back the same way we had come. From the traps I took some more beavers. One place I had to portage, canoe and all. We camped where we slept the first night out. From there I paddled all the way home along the shore.

It was a very pleasant trip for me and my son Ernest. Every day he sat in the canoe in front of me as I paddled along. Once in a while, we scared a fish, who would take off with a big splash, and I would feel the canoe shake a bit. Ernest was not used to sudden noise. I was like that too when we first came to Sibbeston Lake and Dad took me with him on a trip around the lake. I'd sit ahead of him in the boat, and sometimes he'd work late. I'd get sleepy and all of a sudden, splash; that would make me jump nearly out of the boat.

One place we saw a moose feeding along the shore. I told Ernest: "There is a moose ahead."

"Daddy, don't scare him away, I want to see him at close range."

I paddled up to him from behind. Real close. Soon he turned and saw two strangers sitting in a canoe; he ran away from us.

When we came home, Ernest told his mother we saw a moose, and the moose had a piece of old rope around his neck, some of the rope hanging down from the neck. Yes, the moose has something like a rope hanging from the neck, but it is not a rope. It is his cowbell and that's part of him.

I shot and trapped sixteen beavers on this trip, some rats, too, so here I had more work to do, stretching my beavers. I made one final trip to the traps after that, hanging them up on trees where I had used them. By that time I had quite a load to take when we went to the Mackenzie River, so I made one trip alone to the river with thirty-two dried beaver pelts.

When I came back, everybody got ready to leave the lake. I put away all of my winter gear and we left. After sloshing in the boggy muskeg for three days, we were there: Mackenzie River and on to Simpson.

Concluding, I want to leave these few words of advice with you. Some people say they have no job and nothing to do. Others say when we work for our ownselves, we don't get paid because there is no boss; being our own boss, we cannot pay ourselves.

Now, *listen* you, to me. Get this and get it straight. Life is work. If you have a son, there is work for you. Youth is forever demanding guidance, and doing that is work. Yes it is a big job, but it has been done and proved that it can be done.

And now, the other one. When we work we have a boss, he tells us what to do, pays us when we finish the job. If you work for the Power Commission, you'd have a boss; if for the Mission, you'd have a boss. A boss for every work, but every boss is the same. He pays only when the work is finished, not before. And like I said, life is work, and there is a boss for this work, but like other bosses He cannot pay before the job is finished, so if we work hard and well for Him, I am sure He will not deny us our pay, don't you think so too?

2
Moose Hunting on the Mountains

Well, last time we met, it was spring. Now it is late in the fall. A very light snow is on the ground, but the weather is very pleasant, and this time of year, everyone gets the urge to go walking into the woods. I am the same. Of course, I live in the bush, but I get the fever just the same.

A hawk chasing a bird through the woods, a squirrel, the jittery acrobat of the forest, running up and down trees, collecting acorns for the winter . . . yes, it is nice to be out in natural surroundings, but any day from now the north wind will come screaming through the woods, bringing snow and cold.

From here, I know it will be hard driving all the way till winter is done. Comes May, and then it's time to put my driving licence away till next winter. But enough of that for now, and I will get to my story.

Our fish for that winter were already up and Sibbeston Lake was frozen over, ice strong enough to cross on, so we left home

that day, loaded down with our hunting gear and ambition, brother Henry and I.

First day, nothing; second day, nothing, but we were going to the mountains and the first two days were spent getting there. Third day, we got there before dinner and we began to go up, up the ridge that runs down from the mountains. Halfway to the mountain, we went down one side to the low place where a merry brook ran, got some water and made tea.

Right after lunch, we were off again up, up . . . we did not go far before we saw moose, four of them, way out in the distance. Too far from here to shoot them. We fired two rounds of shells over them into the mountains, the bullets hitting rocks on the mountainside. Some rocks loosened and started to roll down the side, and sure enough, one moose got up, started to run this way, towards us, followed by number two, three, four, till there were no more moose to come.

We got them when they got within range, and we skinned and cut away all the rest of the day.

The mountainside is good country. Rugged, solid, rocky

terrain. No trees, just scrub growth, about kneehigh. Just like the kind you see in western films, but no cowboys.

Next day at breakfast, I saw a sheep going along the mountain, so we went that way to the valley that we knew. It was still early in the morning, and all the time we heard moose calling and the rattle of horns. Because we were in low places, we could not see them till we got there and climbed a hill. From the summit of this hill, we looked and what I saw nearly popped my eyes out of their sockets. Biggest concentration of moose I ever saw. Not far from our vantage point, there were nine in one bunch, so we decided to go to this nearest bunch. We didn't go far, one moose began to run. Henry said something I didn't understand, so I leaned over. "Get that one standing over there," he said. I fired three shells, but nothing. I had misjudged the distance, so I lowered my aim. This time I heard the softnosed 30-30 bullet striking home and I knew I got my moose. Henry also shot one, so we skinned and cut them.

When we finished, we covered the meat well. Ready to go, we looked but no moose. I took a stick and hit a horn beside me. Soon a moose got up, two moose, three, four, five, six, seven, eight, nine, ten – moose everywhere. One horned fellow started to walk away, followed by number two, three, four . . . ten. Strings of them going away, in one there were seventeen, and that made quite a long train that disappeared beyond the distant hill.

We went back to our camp and spent the night there. Next day I sharpened our axe well and began to make a big stage for the meat. Henry packed some of the meat to this stage till I finished, then I helped him. By noon, everything was at the stage. We had our lunch and then started to pile the meat on stage. First a layer of meat, then a layer of willows, meat, willows, meat, till everything was up. We took all the hides and covered the top with that, lashed down good.

We camped here again, roasting two ribs so we would have cooked meat supply for next two, three days. Next morning, we packed up and were off again. This time going south till dinner time along the mountain, where we saw white sheep. I went after the sheep, telling Henry to come if he heard me shoot. The sheep got away, but I didn't want to come back; so, I kept climbing, heading for the highest point. I was a bit out of wind when I made the summit.

A feeling that defies description swept over me as I stood there alone and surveyed the wonders of creation. There, stretched out before me from my very feet to the distant blue horizon, were rolling hills, lakes, rivers, valleys, trees, open spaces. A very good, high place to yodel down to someone below, but I

didn't do it. Maybe some day I will go back there just to do that, eh? Good idea!

I started my way down and met Henry about halfway. We found a big boulder there on the mountainside and we decided to give it a kick. So we got behind it with our backs to the mountain and pushed it off with our feet. Slowly at first, it rolled, then it gained speed and came crashing into a patch of stunted trees way down below. Crazy, eh? We're supposed to be hunting. We hunted and found another big boulder, and we gave it the same treatment.

Reaching our packs where we had left them, we went away from the mountain, saying goodbye to the hills. We're supposed to be hunters, not hillbillies. Night overtook us before we went far, so we camped there. For the next two days, we kept travelling on frozen muskeg to Sibbeston Lake and home.

We did not take dogs with us on this hunting trip because dogs make too much noise and moose is easily alarmed. Later on during the winter, when we wanted meat, we went back there and brought back something to eat by dog team.

Next time I write, I will tell you some tricks of my trade. You see, every animal, from the biggest bull moose down to the smallest, meek little mouse, has a way of calling others of his own kind during running season of that particular species. They all understand the call, and respond to it.

Finishing my story, I want to leave a thought and a question with you. All of us come in this world poor and depart from it poor. Others come, live twenty-five, thirty years, acquire a vast, encyclopedic knowledge. Get big. Make a name for themselves. Get classed as immortals and live forever in the pages of history that goes clean down through the ages. You find them in sports, politics, etc. But look, we do not all come here to be big. We cannot conquer the world or something like that. The world is big and we're small, but we could always try and leave some impressions on it. Good impressions. If we do that well enough, maybe we will get a promotion from the big Boss Himself someday. Don't you think so, too?

3
Inviting a Moose for a Picture

Well, I wonder what you think about my experiences that I have been telling you about? Maybe you think I made them up, maybe you think I'm bragging too much. No! These were my actual experiences, that I had lived through. Sure, I had some unpleasant experiences too, some close shaves. But a guy could always profit by learning from these bad experiences too. Life in the bush is not easy, but nothing in life is easy. Many times I have gone to bed without supper in weather thirty below, not because I was bad, but I made mistakes. So you see, this is not the life of Riley, but I have gone thus far, learned a few things through understanding, acquired a fair amount of knowledge about this kind of life, and I have the scorched pants to prove it. Scorched from being too close to campfires of the bush trails . . .

Enough of this for now. Let's look into the diary.

September, 1957 and we were back at our winter camp at Sibbeston Lake. We wanted to put up some fish for the winter, so we got our canoes loaded and left home. My brother Henry

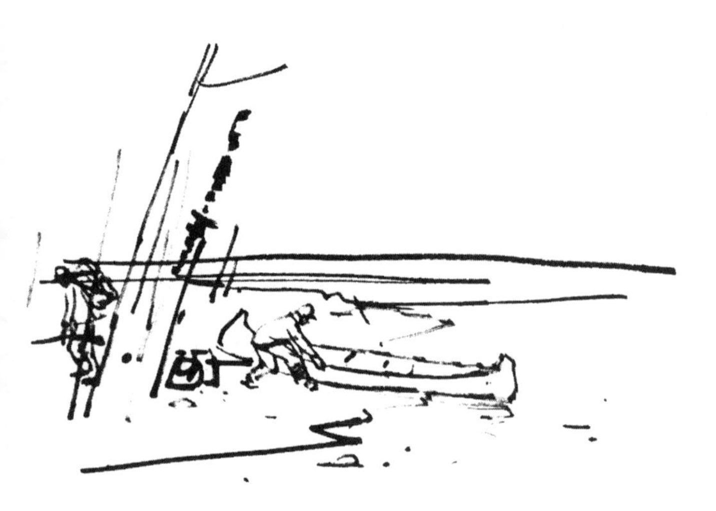

and I in one canoe, George Cli, a brother-in-law, in the other canoe. About an hour from home, while crossing a bay, we saw a moose wading out in the lake. George had a camera loaded with colour film, so we decided to take a picture of the moose. We all paddled that way. We did not go far and saw two more moose come out of the bush.

We were still a little way when they all walked back into the bush. We landed there on the shore and pulled up our canoes and walked from there. When we got within hearing distance of them, we decided to make the bull come to us for his picture. I had a piece of flat bone, shaped like a short paddle with a handle, and I was going to use that to make him come. George had the camera, so he came next to me.

The bush was so thick, but we found a little clearing where the sunshine filtered in and we selected the spot for our shot. I rubbed my bone hard against a tree. A little way in the thicket a tree started swinging hard, back and forth, and we heard his horns being rubbed against a tree. After a minute, he stopped. I called him and he called me too. I used the bone again and he used his horns. I called and he called. On and on we called each other, I and the bull moose. Between calls I used the bone and he used his horns. Every time he rubbed a tree, it was a different one. We could see it swinging and noted that the moose was coming our way all the time, though we couldn't see him yet.

Soon, he was near our clearing, which was about twenty feet across, and I kept on calling him till he came into the clearing and stood there for his picture. For a second or two I had a funny, topsy-turvy feeling inside of me as I stood there facing the bull moose. He was standing only yards away, with his big, wicked-looking horns and no sign of friendship in his eyes.. What a ticklish situation I got myself into, just to satisfy a fisherman turned photographer.

After a while, I looked at the cameraman out of the corner of my eyes, and saw him put the camera down and pick up the rifle. Soon, he fired and the bull went down. We passed the bull, went after the cow and calf. I still had my flat bone and was going to use it on the cow too, but I guess she heard the shot. I saw them running away, but I couldn't shoot, bush being too thick. With the speed that they went, I figured they could be south of the border that same day.

Well, we got one moose and one picture, which did not turn out too good, but the meat was good. We cut up all the meat, cached it good, and went to our fishery.

4 Rabbit Hunting

Way back in 1942, I bought my first .22 rifle from Herb Kerr, a white trapper, in town. Day after we got home, I took my shooting iron down to the mouth of Trail creek and took it all apart, examined it, put it back together. Then I loaded it with shells, pumped one into the firing chamber, aimed it and pulled the trigger. It worked well.

Next day a gang of us guys went rabbit hunting. I didn't know how to call rabbits, so I asked one of my friends. He said that I could learn it from the rabbits. I asked him how and he told me. So I took my gun and walked into the bush. I did not go far and I ran into a litter of young baby rabbits. I chased one that seemed as though it would never stop, but finally I caught it. The little rabbit started crying, producing a long kissing-like sound. Soon, an adult rabbit came running out of the woods, circling me. Very soon, another one, and then another one. Three rabbits and I got two out of three.

I let the little rabbit go, walked a little way and called, making sounds just like that little rabbit. Sure enough, rabbits came running from all directions, five of them. I put two of them in my pack.

All morning, I walked through the woods. Every so often I stopped to call and pick some, till I had quite a load, then I went back to the starting point to find the gang all there, feasting on rabbits.

Nearly every day we went rabbit hunting back in those days. Rabbits were plentiful then. This is in the month of June of that year. On one of these hunts, Frank Cli got lost, and stayed in the bush for more than twelve hours. Wind was blowing hard and we all split up in pairs, walking through woods, calling for Frank. Comes ten o'clock in the evening, but no Frank, so we went home, thinking maybe he found an old trail and went home on it. When we got home, nobody had seen him, so back we went. We looked and searched, covering about four miles. We worked all afternoon, all night till eight o'clock next morning when we went back to the river, tired. We made tea and had something to eat and were ready to go again, when we saw someone coming along the shore. When he came up, it was Frank all right, tired. Ten o'clock we went home, and to bed I went.

Well to some of the readers these things that I do seem rather cruel, I know that too, but I don't have a warehouse full of grub with me all the time, and I got to get it from the bush.

5 How the Mackenzie River Was Made

(Translation of a Slavey Legend)

Way back in the days of bow and arrow, we had spring, summer, fall and winter, just like we have now. One year, we do not know what year it was, something went wrong. It was spring now, and the pretty leaves were on the trees. The birds of every kind came from the South, built their nests and laid their eggs in them. The cow moose had their calves born and hovered over them protectingly. Certain fishes that spawn in the spring went up creeks to do the work of reproduction.

The people put away their snowshoes, moved their camps to sunny hillsides, and took it easy, soaking up the sun. Their hard, cold winter days were over, and long, lazy days were here. Little did they know what nature had in store for them.

One morning, they awoke to find a little snow on the ground and cold. The north wind was blowing hard and more snow was coming down. Soon, everything was covered with a heavy blanket

of snow. Lakes froze over, and some waterfowl perished, being caught unprepared. There were rivers, but they were small ones. These rivers too froze, and the water ceased to run in them.

At first people thought it strange, it made some of them laugh, some thought it might be just a late spring snowfall. Soon, they were forced to put their snowshoes on, as more snow kept coming down and by now was kneedeep.

On and on it snowed, the wind also kept whistling through the woods, piling huge drifts many feet deep. After many days, the wind died down, and the snow ceased to fall. A very bitter cold gripped the land under its blanket of white. The days grew shorter, just like when it's winter, with long, long cold nights.

Across the vast land, starvation stalked both man and beast. Some villages were lucky, others were not. Once in a while, someone found a frozen calf given up by the mother, but a little calf in a large village was not enough to keep everyone alive, and soon some villages had no smoke coming from them.

The great Master knew the suffering of the poor people, so He decided on a plan to help them, and at the same time made a big river for us, to drink from, to fish in, and travel on. As the people in those days ate mostly meat, our Master sent them a great big ball of dried meat, which dropped somewhere in the east from here. When it dropped, the huge ball started to roll westward. Two young men in white garments (angels) were also sent. These men had long poles with a spear at one end, and as the great ball rolled they attacked it with their poles, peeling great chunks of the dried meat.

When the man on the left peeled some off, he attacked with such vigour, it made the huge ball roll more to the right and it did the same with the man on the right, winding as our river does today. Instead of decreasing in size as some of it was being peeled off, the great ball grew bigger and bigger as it rolled across the land and into the sea, thus making the river wider towards the mouth.

A great, wide path was left where the huge ball had rolled, leaving no trees standing. People hunting in the woods came upon this path, some of them were frightened away, thinking some monster was roaming the land, eating people. Others were braver and walked along the wide path finding peeled-off meat. Soon, word was spread and people moved their camps to this strip of broken land. Every day, people gathered the meat, storing it away.

Many, many moons later, the days grew longer and warmer. By and by, spring came again, and with spring, the birds came back from the South. The snow on the mountains and trees

melted, turned into water and made the little rivers come back to life with the merry sound of running water.

Gradually, the wide path filled up with water from the melting snow, and started to flow in the direction taken by the big ball of meat. At first it was awfully muddy, but as time went on, it got clearer, and as it did all the broken trees were carried away to the mouth.

Many winters and summers later, white men started to come into the country, discovering lakes and rivers, and naming them. One such white man came and got the big river named after him, but we were here before he came and we know this much more about the Mackenzie than he does!

6 Going through the Wringer

I have been pretty busy during the month of May: been to North Nahanni three times, two trips into town, built a speedboat, visited at Willow River, and here I go again, to reminisce a bit with you once more. By the way, what do you think about that Mackenzie story? Maybe one of you could have a better version of that Mackenzie legend! If so, I suggest that you take it down in writing, submit it for publication. You know, the hardest part of this is getting the ball rolling.

Yes, I know there is talent lying dormant somewhere, waiting for that special call. Myself, I am not a writer, singer, artist, or anything like that.

My thinking is not so good, my education limited. So, if you find a word misspelled or misplaced, it is because I have these drawbacks, but I guess I will cut this short for now, and let myself dig into the diary for the black pages of it.

I mean to tell you about some of the unfortunate experiences that man, including myself, goes through. Catching the expression, we will say "going through the wringer".

My first red letter day was way back in those days when we were allowed ten beavers. Regulation forbids shooting them too, so we had to pack traps. We had eight traps, my partner, Henry Doctor, now dead, and I. We had crossed the big, rough candy mountain into the North Nahanni valley, where we planned to go down one of the tributaries of North Nahanni.

But once it gains momentum, it can roll just like the ball of meat in that Mackenzie story.

We already had caught our full quotas of ten beavers each, but muskrats were fairly thick and we wanted to take as many as we could. We camped between a river and the lake that Peter Mckeown used to call Sixty-Mile Lake. Sixty miles from the mouth, that is. The muskrats of this lake soon thinned out and we drifted down the river. Nice, lazy river for the first day, but being familiar with the country, we knew we would have rough going on the second. We camped there on the edge of the rough waters and next day, drifted down nearly all the way through the bad spot till the last point.

Here the river had formed a new channel, leaving a dead point. We landed ashore, walked over and took a look. Lots of broken

trees, roots and fast rough water. From the other side, a long thin pole stuck halfway across, just inches above water. We went back to our canoes and I pushed off to lead the way. To my surprise, I found out that most of the water ran under that skinny old pole, but I figured it might bend and break off when I got pushed against it. It did not break or bend at all, it tipped me and the canoe over instead, and into the drink I went. I had my legs stretched out under a crossbar of the canoe and I had quite a time kicking my heels free, but I finally did. I reached out and caught the keel, which was now on top, and hung on. I drifted well past the choppy waters and swam ashore. My canoe was floating by not too far out, so I ran down after it. I went into the river again, got it, and pulled it in. Trapped air in it made it so hard for me to have it righted.

Every time I tried to lift one end, the whole river seemed to go with it. I could not move fast. My clothes were wet and I was hindered by that. I had two dogs, one had jumped clear, the one must be drowning under that canoe. I pulled and lifted. After much labouring, I got it righted, my poor dog floated out dead. I took it ashore and tied the canoe. Then I told my friend to take a box of matches, take some out, put small rocks in it to add weight and throw it across. He did, and it fell into the river.

He went back to his canoe and managed to go through the tight spot, landed below and we got a fire going. I took all my clothes off, wrung them, hung them by the fire, dried and I put them on. I had lost all my heavy equipment, one dog, my axe, my rifles, two knives, over twelve cartons of .22 shells (a carton holds five hundred). These were intended for future use and I was going to put them in the shack that we had out there. All my light goods, bedroll, dried beaver skins and muskrats floated and drifted ashore, and we picked them up as we went.

We also dismantled one of the canoes, which were just roughly made affairs and were rather clumsy to maneuver in tight places. So, from here, we used one boat to go sixty miles. Lucky for me, my companion also had two .22 rifles and he supplied me with the shells too, so I was shooting high all the way, just like nothing had happened.

My next May day comes years later on the trail from Sibbeston Lake. I had finished my spring work, made one trip to the river with my spring catch, and now I was taking my family with me. We usually make it in three days of steady going, but on this trip, we were caught by the rain. First it was just a light drizzle, then it started to come heavy, coming down in buckets. I put up a shelter, made a fire and we settled down to sit out the rain.

The storm lasted three days and on the fourth day, clouds began to break and no rain. We were not prepared for so many days on the trail, so our food supply had been exhausted. We packed up and resumed our march to our destination. All the creeks were swollen with the rainwater overflowing their banks, and we had to cross six of them. I made a bridge across every creek till the last one, which was only half an hour from the river.

We stopped, and I got out of my harness, the tumpline, looked the situation over, and I got my axe to make the bridge. I felled two trees that reached the other side, but when I laid them side by side, they made a pretty narrow bridge. Too risky to take my family treasure across on that. So, I cut another tree which stops halfway, I worked it loose and it went down to stop again. I was thinking of cutting it free, but just then I happened to be at the wrong place at the wrong time. The tree broke off its holding wood and took a swing at me, which caught me flush on the chest and I was thrown ten feet backwards, landing on the wet moss.

I got up, but I was kind of wobbly so I sat down again. My chest began to hurt like the dickens and I felt something coming up my throat. I coughed and when I did, I really felt the pain. I spat out the thing, which turned out to be blood. I sat there, spitting blood that comes up.

Jane had run to my side and cried a bit, which did not help matters any. She now got me some water and I washed my throat and mouth, drinking some. After half an hour the pain eased down somewhat and I got my axe and cleared the limbs off the bridge that spanned the creek. One by one I took my family

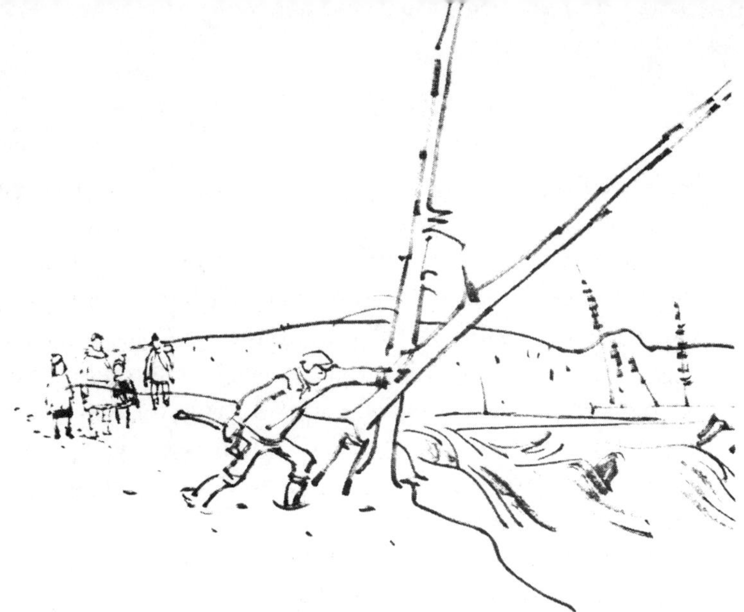

across. Two of my dogs fell into the foamy torrent and were carried downstream by the fast-moving waters. I thought they'd be goners but they came back, one without his pack. I saw them go, but I could not run after them. I had to avoid any quick movements on account of the pain.

We reached the river that evening and camped in our house. Next day we went across the river to the village, and I got Frank Cli and Edward Horesay to run the kicker to take us to town. I went to see Doctor Nyhus next day. He said I had a broken chestbone and told me to do absolutely no heavy work for one full month. I did and my chestbone never bothered me at all afterwards.

Accidents like these always happen when you don't expect them. If and when they do happen, the best medicine is to stay coolheaded, don't get excited and comes sea or high water, you will stay above water. This is sound, solid advice. Not all of my misfortunes were accidents of this nature. I have some pretty bad mistakes made sometimes, and that taught me many a good lesson. Of course, in life there is many a slip, and I have taken some pretty bad pills too.

Just only last winter one day, after telling Jane I'd be away for five days, I loaded my toboggan and left. I had planned to visit some of my beaver colonies up the creek and maybe have a payload to take home. My food ran out on the third day, but I was camping by a live lodge and expected to catch one beaver next morning. Early next day I went to see my traps but had caught zero, nothing. I was in good chicken country, lots of jackpines with ridges.

I took out my .22 rifle and got ready to hunt. Unfortunately, my toboggan had rubbed against trees coming up, tore a hole through the canvas wrapper and my pack, through which my box of shells had fallen out, unnoticed. I hitched my dogs, started back in the afternoon, hungry as a pig. I stopped at my next two traps and went over to see them. One trap had sprung, without even a hair in it. I went over to the next one and found it gone. I took another good hard look and really it was gone. I had caught a beaver, but it did not drown, came out of the hole I punched, walked a bit in the snow, and dove back in, taking my trap with it.

My heart sank, together with my spirits. After a while I began to think better and walked around some. There was a heavy pool of water where I had my trap out, with two narrow passages where the beaver could go in and out. I punched a hole and poked around one way; nothing. I poked the other way and felt wood. I made the hole bigger and cleaned out the ice chips with a frying pan. I pushed up my shirt sleeve and got my hand into the icy waters, feeling for that wood. I felt it, so I pulled. It was hard, but I had it dislodged somehow and yanked it out. My trap pole, my trap and a dead beaver. Yippee! I'm all right! I rolled and pulled it in the snow, taking the water out of its fur.

I dragged it back to my camp and made fire. I didn't bother skinning it, I just cut it open, took out the liver and cooked it on a pointed stick. I cut the tail off too, took the scaly matter off, and cooked it too. I got myself some snow and made my tea. By this time I was so hungry I could almost chew my nails off my fingers. My cooking was done, so I ate and felt a lot better. Believe me, that simple meal of cooked liver and tail tasted great! To me, it was something far better and tastier than those hundred-dollar plates you hear about in a big political convention. I have never tasted those plates, and I guess I never will, but I think my little meal had them pretty well beaten that day. Why, I did not even cook it according to the recipe of the cookbook! But I am not a very rich man and can't afford one anyway. Yes, you never know how good the necessities of life are till you miss them like I did.

Next time, I will tell about my broken-down rifle on a spring hunt, many miles away from civilization, so keep posted, will you?

7
Repairing a Broken Rifle

Here I go again, lamenting about the heyday of the trapper, who makes money but has a million ways of spending it. I remember the good years when beaver used to sell well, back in the fifteen-beavers days. That was when dad first let me take the reins. I was twenty-seven then. I have taken the good and the bad but always hoping for a brighter tomorrow.

I remember one bad year when our trapping season started with a dozen wolves hanging around our camp. They were so bad for two months till I dispatched some of them. Other fellows caught some too, thirteen of them altogether. I will tell later on about that, but now it's time to put the broken pieces of my rifle together. So, let's see how it can be done.

Starting from Sibbeston Lake, we had gone through a pass in the mountain, and were in the North Nahanni valley. We generally go here if we plan a big catch because it is good beaver country. It is mostly water, lakes and rivers.

This was spring and travel was mostly in water, by pack. Dogs also had packs. Some are long-legged and these usually packed the blankets. Being long-legged, they keep the blankets well out of the water. Sometimes we treat the pack with melted tallow, waterproofing it.

There were three of us on this hunting expedition, my brother Fred, Jim Horesay, an uncle, and I. Uncle Jim died years later, but then he was the oldest man and acted as a leader for the group.

Muskrats were pretty thick that year, but between my brother and I, we had a 25-20, which was too big to use on muskrats, and one .22. I had the smaller rifle, but some days we changed guns. One day, it was his turn to have the .22 and he left the camp early. I left too, and stayed all the afternoon, coming back late in the evening. A big fire was roaring at camp when I was approaching and I could almost smell trouble before I was told that my .22 rifle had broken down. Our older brother, Jimmy, and another fellow were hunting in the same area and we met just a few days before. So, there was a gang of five good hunters, one with a broken gun.

Next day, they allowed me to set all their traps. Everybody took pity on me, you see! My rifle broken and I could not go on hunting foray into the bush. That afternoon, everyone went hunting except me. I stayed at camp and had nothing to do but think, and I really thought hard too. The little gun had kept me busy before, but it was broken now, and I felt I was a member of the gang no more. I felt pretty lonely, alone with my thoughts.

That day, Fred and Jim went in pair and when they came back in the evening, they had a big, old file that they had found. They said they had found an old camp and looked it over, and that is where they found the file.

Charlie Cholo and his friends used to come here to hunt before the registered area went into effect. Maybe my good friend Charlie had left the file there for me. But I think he must have forgotten it. Next day we took the broken gun apart. This was a single shot, bolt action kind, which had to be cocked for firing. This cocking piece acts as a hammer by spring action and hits the firing pin to shoot the gun. The hammer was in one long piece about five inches, but when we took it out, it came out in two pieces, broken.

We examined it, thinking maybe we could put it together somehow. We found that it couldn't be done, so we turned our attention to the old file. If we hammered and filed it into shape, it might work, but a lot of hammering and filing would have to be done. We decided to use the old file and throw away the broken pieces. But first we had to use it as a pattern for the new piece we were going to make, so we kept the two pieces.

First, we had to take the temper out of it, which makes it brittle and that resists filing. So, we stuck it into a piece of green log and put it into the coals. Soon it got hot and Jimmy started hammering it between two axes. We took turn doing the hammering, which lasted nearly all that day.

Next day we filed it, tried it for fit and filed it some more. After a good day of filing, we laid it alongside the broken pieces put together, and it looked nearly alike. We filed a bit more and tried it in place. With a metallic click that was music to my ears, the thing slipped into position without any effort and I was excited, jubilant. We got a shell in the chamber and tried to pull it back to cock it into firing position. It was hard, the spring being rather strong. Besides, we had filed it a bit too short and couldn't get a good hold on it.

I filed a groove all around it, tied a piece of string in the groove, made a loop in it, got a finger in the loop and pulled.

This time it cocked into firing position. I pointed the business end away from my companions and pulled the trigger. *Bang!*, went the gun and I turned to face my companions to smile for the first time in four days.

That afternoon I went hunting, with a feeling that I was a member of the party. But, believe me, I had done a world of thinking in the short space of four days, that some of you readers could do in a lifetime. After two days of hunting, something else turned up on the same gun. I took it apart again and examined it. Being soft with the temper out of it, the business end where it hits the firing pin had burred badly. The burred edge interfered with its working mechanism.

I had tested my skill before in making special steels and the knowledge will stand me in good stead now. So, I had confidence. I filed off the bad edge, cut a muskrat carcass in half, ran the piece through and applied it to the heat. It got redhot and I dipped it in cold water. When cooled, I hit it lightly with a file at the end. It had that high, vibrating sound of good hard steel. I hit it a little farther up and it had that low, sleepy sound of soft metal. I put the gun together again and tested it and it work better.

My thinking was over for that and I did a splendid hunting, going back to Sibbeston Lake the same way we had come.

Well, it's fun recalling these past experiences for you. I do this because I hope some of you, especially the younger generation, will learn something from my own experiences. Reading is the best form of absorbing information, you know!

8 The Wolf: Number One Enemy

Next month, the trapping season starts again, and I will be busy. I am already getting the fever. The first snow is always welcome. It's lovely, white against the bare ground. Nice to go walking into the woods, seeing tracks of different animals.

By April, I know I will be tired of the snow, which sometimes gets too deep. Some years it is so deep, the moose drags his belly in it, leaving a wide strip of broken snow. Some animals don't travel much then, like the porcupine, which does its travelling in the fall, same time as the moose and caribou. So, it will stay at one place and wait till the snow disappears.

Some years it snows too early and too deep; then it's bad for the trapper all the way till spring. Other years are bad too, like the year that started with wolves around the camp. Wolverine is bad too. But the wolf is number one on my bad list. It will eat its fill and cache what it cannot eat. Sometimes it does not go far to cache the stolen property, so I watch for that. I follow tracks leaving the trail after stealing and sometimes recover the stolen fur. A story circulates among the natives that the wolverine and the marten were great friends, back in the bow and arrow days. True or not, I have never seen the wolverine eat the marten out of a trap. He always caches the marten pulled out of a trap.

One year just recently, I caught a wolverine on the trail to Sibbeston Lake. George Cli and I were going to the lake, with me bringing up the rear. The wolverine pulled himself free and started to run ahead on the trail. Boy! we had a wild ride that lasted one full hour, till the wolverine climbed a tree and we brought it down with a .22. Some dog teams are hard to hold when dogs pick up the scent of fresh moose tracks or something like that.

The bad year that I remember was not too long ago, when wolves were thick. At first they were not so hungry because the weather was mild, but then it turned cold, real cold. I made several trips to the traps but I never brought anything home. I also had a snare line for rabbits which was rendered useless to me by the wolves. Every two days I went and repaired the broken rabbit snares. I was disappointed at the end of the first month with nothing to show for that time. I decided to get after the wolves before I make another trip to the traps. So I moved my camp one day away and set some rabbit snares close by. I also set one trap for wolf on both ends of this snare line. Trail sets.

Next day I went to see my snares and traps. My first trap was only about a hundred yards from my camp. When I got there, it was gone. So I followed the trapped wolf by the tracks which led away from camp. He dragged my trap about a hundred yards, got tangled up in some bushes, and all that was left of him was his tail and one foot still in the trap. I took the trap back to the trail and put it there, planning to reset on my return. My snares were broken again, so I kept going to my next trap. When I reached it, I had to hunt for it awhile before I found it. The foot of a wolf in it . . . I set it in the same place and went back. I fixed all the snares and set the other trap.

Next day, the story was repeated. Some nights I didn't catch any. Some other nights I caught two; other times only one. If I did catch one or two in a night, all that was left could be the tail, as other wolves would come and eat them.

By and by the tracks became fewer, and those that I caught were left intact, so I knew they were losing their number. By the end of the second month there were no wolves except one. This wolf was smart and I couldn't catch him. I tried different tricks and he did the same. Finally, he kind of minded his own business, though he still hung around. Somebody else caught this one later in the winter. I had been counting them and the last one was number thirteen.

Wolves that hang around are usually old ones that are too old to hunt for themselves. Their teeth are worn short, maybe from chewing bones. Sibbeston Lake is good for wolves, as the hills are close to the lake. Moose come to the lake from the hills and wolves follow them, but these hunting wolves never bother us. Sure some odd one will come to stay for a while, but we either catch or shoot them. One summer I saw one going across the river. I was in a canoe with a kicker, and I am sure I did not hesitate to pick up my rifle and send that one down the river, dead.

One bad wolf on a trapline is just as bad as many. One such wolf stayed two winters at Sibbeston Lake. Sure we were all out for him and caught him many times, but he always managed to free himself. Soon, he learned and got so smart it was almost impossible to get rid of him. He got smart on our

trapline, where he ate part of our catch, then just hung around the fish stage. The stage was not too high and he would stand up on his hind legs and eat heads off the fish.

One day I set about a dozen traps under the stage for him. Two days later, Henry went to get some fish, came back and said there was a wolf in one of the traps. He did not carry a rifle, so I hitched up my team and went to the stage, taking a rifle along. The wolf was just lying in the snow. Funny, I thought, not on his feet. I shot and killed him. Then, I examined him: he had been caught so many times in one front leg, the leg froze up to the elbow, and he had chewed all the flesh off, leaving only the bone. I had caught him by the only good front leg he had. That was why he was not on his feet. I was glad to get rid of that one, but materially and financially, it had done us a lot of damage for two years.

Well, next month I will go trapping the beaver and other fur-bearing animals. Beaver trapping under the ice, that is, and I'll tell you about that. Some people like to tell stories, you know, while others love to listen to part of the things that make our good old world tick, you know!

9
Cold Chills over Bears

Well, it's here at last, snow on the ground and trapping season. The wind flowing on the face and the smell of campfire smoke are two temptations I can't resist . . . and the good solid feeling that you are your own boss. Yes, I'm going to take it, whether it will be a good or bad winter. Some people like to complain a lot for little things, but not me. I figure it's part of life and take it with a smile. But this life as a bushman is not a bed of roses, I can tell you that.

In all my wanderings in the woods, the only animal I have come to fear is the bear. A bear once clawed my grandfather up pretty badly. He had wounded the bear and followed it. Suddenly, the bear came out of the bush towards Grandpa. He took aim and pulled the trigger. The hammer clicked on an empty cartridge case. He had forgotten to pump a fresh shell in. By this time, the bear was upon him, clawing and biting. Somehow, the bear left him again after nearly scratching one eye out, face torn away and bleeding badly. He managed to find his gun and make it back to

the river. He was brought into town soon after and received treatment in the hospital. I was in school in Providence then and only heard the story later.

One spring on a beaver hunt, a friend of mine shot a bear two hundred yards from our camp. I was away and he waited till I came back. Then, we both went over to the bear, leaving our rifles at camp. I was in the lead and we walked right up to the bear. We were about to turn it over when I noticed something funny. I have seen dead ones before, but this one had his teeth bared. I had the axe, so I gave the bear a blow on the head with the back of the axe. The bear screamed and started to kick. Two more blows, this time with the blade, and I cut off the head. We nearly tried to skin him alive and it was only after I had finished him off that I got the cold chills.

10
Beaver Hunting Tricks

Enough of this for now because I don't want to scare you away, so I can tell you about my beaver traps and how I set them. First, I have to find the beaver house, which is made of mud and sticks. The feed pile is usually in front of the lodge and varies in size according to the size of the beaver family. If I find a lodge, I go hitting the ice with the back of my axe along the shoreline. The trained human ear can be something like the electronic flaw-detector used in the steel industry. It will detect flaws in the ice, air bubbles left to freeze in the ice by the beavers as they go in and out of holes in the mud banks. So, as I go along the shore, hitting with my axe, I listen for that special music. If I hear it, I punch a hole with my ice chisel, and if there is a runway, pieces of green cut logs can also be noticed, imbedded in the ice. No bark on them. To make sure there is a runway, I use what I might call a feeler-stick. This is a long, curved stick, something like a bow under full strain, but longer than the bow. With this, I poke the shoreline, feeling along. If there is a runway,

I go and cut some green poles in lengths according to the depth of the water. I also cut a dry pole, which is going to hold the trap by going through the ring at the end of the trap chain. This pole has to be a dry one or the beaver will cut it off and take it away, and maybe I will lose the trap. I clean the ice chips out of the punched hole as these interfere with the effective setting of the trap. I take the green logs now and push them down hard into the bottom, making a kind of a pen. Then, I take a thin pole, make the end pointed and set my trap. I dip it first in the water to give it a coating of ice. The pointed end of the pole also gets a dipping. The pointed end now goes into the hole of the trap spring where the jaws go. I lower the contraption in, the trap always hitting bottom first. The pole with the trap chain attached has to be pushed hard into the bottom. The dipping of the trap and the pointed pole is done to prevent them from sticking fast together as they get in contact with water. Now I take that pointed pole out of the trap, which is now all set for business. This is a very effective set and I always use that kind of set. I also set other traps in other places.

Maybe I will camp here for two nights and look around for more beaver lodges and by that time the beaver should have been around the traps. Sometimes I catch only the toenail, which the beaver loses to me, and if I do, that beaver will never be caught in a trap. The trap springing in the water also makes a noise which the beaver hears, and being a smart animal, it will not repeat the same mistake again. Traps set in front of the lodge are good too, but most likely will catch a little beaver. The size counts big in marketing the beaver pelt.

Spring beaver trapping is different; of course, in open water I much prefer to shoot them. You see, I use the meat as much as the hide, and a shot beaver tastes good, especially when I'm hungry. Even with a good hunter, the beaver can and will slip away. Like one spring, I ran into two beavers in a pool of water only about fifty feet across. The water was not deep and only one narrow passage led out of that pool. I went over to this narrow passage, where the water was only about eight inches deep, and thought I was going to get them as they left the pool of water. This was in broad daylight and they kept diving back in as they came out. Soon, I noticed one coming towards me under the shallow water. He made a sharp turn, kicking up dirt from the bottom. They both went to work, kicking up dirt and soon I could not see through that eight inches of water. Soon too, everything was still, no sign at all of the two beavers that I thought I was going to skin. They had slipped away out of the passage right under my very feet, and I didn't see them at all. Beaver under shallow water never move fast, and these two pulled a pretty slick one on me that time.

11
Christmas on the Trapline

Christmas day on the trapline, like in any other place, passes quickly. Too quickly sometimes, it seems. I have many pleasant recollections of the past Christmasses, which were all white ones. I mean the ever-present snow. It dates back to the days when I was at school at Fort Providence, where we were taught the true meaning of Christmas. But, this is all about Christmas on the trapline, and, to illustrate what I mean, I will tell you about two of these past Christmasses.

The first white Christmas that I remembered on the trapline was back in the year of 1938. There was Dad, Fred and I. We had left home, gone through the mountains by a pass, and were on the other side. We had made one trip here before and had traps scattered here and there.

On the evening of the twenty-fourth, we had travelled late. It was about ten o'clock when we had made our fire. This is common on the line. Breakfast is big, because we don't stop for dinner; sometimes we do, but rarely. At times we start at eight

and finish at ten in the night. On this particular trip, we had to, because we had a stage that we wanted to reach that night. We camped there by the stage.

It was one of those clear, cold nights, and the aurora borealis put on a magnificent display of white, roving fingers across the night sky as we lay in our beddings, waiting to catch our forty winks, the campfire dying low towards the feet. We were quite tired and slipped into dreamland. Mountain travel is unlike that of flat country. It is up slowly and down fast.

Christmas morning bright and early, we packed up and hitched up the dogs, seven of them in two teams, and we're off again. This was our way back towards home, through the pass. The pass is through a canyon and at first, we used snowshoes, then the snow got lighter as we came up higher. We put our snowshoes on the toboggans and ran after the dogs, holding the head rope.

There are caves in this canyon, and some old people say the boss of the winds lived there. If a loud noise is made close to the cave, he gets mad and makes a big wind blow hard. We passed here many times before and sometimes we shot our rifles into the caves, but we never woke up that boss of the winds. Now as we pass below the caves, some of them appeared to be yawning, but no wind. Maybe too early, or maybe because it's Christmas day.

It took us four hours to go through the mountain, not seeing a bird or anything.

On the other side, just on the edge of the timber, we had caught a fox. We surely had a dandy time, trying to hold back the dogs. No trees at all to stop them and the snow was firmly packed by the winds. Bald hills on the sides of the mountain are always windswept. Many times we see sheep coming through the pass, sometimes we go after the sheep. They always go where we cannot follow them.

From here, it's light timber all the way to Sibbeston Lake. We kept going all that Christmas day, not stopping for dinner. Sometimes we saw whisky-jacks, but that was all we saw that Christmas day.

We made our camp early and fed our dogs. We had been travelling all that Christmas day, seeing mostly trees of different kinds, and muskegs covered now with snow. The mountain air feels clean, with a light breeze blowing against the face and the snow-covered trees swaying gently in the wind. The mountain is long, running south, and it's big and rough, no place for a tenderfoot.

That night, an owl came from somewhere and hooted nearby. The northern lights came back to play across the sky. We must have stayed up late listening to Dad telling us a story because the Big Dipper was dipping its handle, indicating late hour. We unrolled our beddings and crawled in.

Yes, this was Christmas 1938, right on the trapline, under the stars and northern lights. Others have come and gone, but these were at home. Some are spent in the settlement.

Just last year, at Two Islands where I trap during the winter, Christmas day was spend at home. I had visited my traps and came home on the twenty-fourth. My side of the river is good mainly for marten and lynx, so I trap mostly them. I had a tent one day away from the river. From this tent, I came home and as the days were short, it was already dusk when I walked in. I warmed myself well, fed my dogs and lit the gas lamp.

After supper, I got out some colored streamers and began to decorate our home. In the center of the room, I put up the decoration in the form of a big, five-point star, and worked out from there. Around windows I used strips of coloured crepe paper and around our two doors, too. I will admit I am no expert at this and it took me quite some time to have it done.

After I finished, I turned on the radio, and gosh, the air just seems loaded with Christmas music. Everywhere I turned the dial, it's the same. I pointed the dial to my favourite station, and sure enough, Bing Crosby. Halfway in the program, he came on with the best-loved carols. "Silent Night, Holy Night" came pouring out of the radio. Being a bit on the sentimental side, a little lump formed in my throat. Bing has touched millions of hearts anyway! Later on, we listened to the Midnight Mass somewhere in the east. Past midnight we went to bed.

Christmas day! We put our best clothes on, hitched up our dogs, and went to visit across the river. We went first to my brother Jimmy's place and sat there awhile. Then we all walked out and headed for Cli's place. After the greetings, we sat around to listen to Cli telling a story about old times. I noticed the women being busy around the table and looked at my watch. It was nearly twelve o'clock. Cli finished the story, told everyone to have dinner with him. So we went to the table. We took our seats around the table, which was loaded with food, the best of the house for Christmas. We kept silent for a minute, then someone said something to break the silence, the monotony. Someone else said something funny and everybody burst out laughing.

The table shook in laughter and for a minute or two, I thought it was laughing too! Little ripples in a cup of tea beside me. It turned out that someone sitting across the table had put his big belly against it. Some of our hefty people can really laugh, you know. This one did and created a mystery of the laughing table there for me, right on Christmas day. After dinner, we sat around again, talking.

Soon it was getting dark, so we left for home. Everything was cold when we came in and made a fire. Later in the evening, we switched the radio on for more Christmas music. After a while, the radio said so many people had died, which is rather hard to believe, but I guess it's true. People sometimes try to put everything in one short day, ending in wrong places. Well, I guess it was Christmas not only here, but Christmas all over the world.

Our year's day was spent at the same place, Two Islands, with a visit across. Yes, Christmas 1961 has come and gone, but it will be here again soon.

12 Winter Travelling

When it gets cold in January, everything seems dead, still. If you happened to be living in the bush like me, summer and winter, you will notice that there are two periods in the year when everything seems to stop still. January and June. In January, it gets bitterly cold and animals don't travel much. This is the hardest part of the year to travel by dog team. The toboggan does not run easily and gets iced up badly. Some nicer mornings, dogs could be raring to go, but on January mornings, they seem to shrink at the sight of cold harness.

January the first finds us in Simpson sometimes, me and my brothers. Going home to Sibbeston Lake is just like coming in to Simpson. Snow had covered up the trail and the going is hard. But we take turns plodding ahead. Our loads consist of store-bought goods such as tea, lard, flour, candles, clothes and plugs of chewing tobacco for the folks way out yonder. Days are short and even little things we do seem time-consuming, but we do not live by the clock like the white man anyway!

One year, after our trip to town and a good rest, Dad said we would go to the mountains. It so happened that the weather turned milder. Me and Dad left home first, while Fred and Henry had wood to haul for a day. We went through the mountains on Little Doctor Lake after travelling for two days. (Little Doctor was my grandfather from my mother's side). The green country that we knew wasn't green any more. Summer before, there was a lot of smoke and fire had killed all the trees. We kept going till we found a patch of green spruce and camped.

Next day, Dad said we would wait for Fred and Henry and told me to hunt. I got everything ready: shells, rifle, knife and a packsack. I put on my snowshoes and walked away, leaving Dad at camp. I walked all morning, making a big circle along a river, and soon I saw a moose. He was feeding along the river and I tried to walk up to him, using stealth. I was too much in the open and he saw me coming and took off in the opposite direction. I was going in that particular direction too, so I followed him by the tracks. About a mile from camp, I caught up with my moose in the thickest bush you can imagine and I did a lot of shooting. My gun was pretty hot to the touch when he went down in the snow and I walked up to him.

It was not late in the day, so I just cut the head off and started back to camp. Fred and Henry were with Dad at camp when I came. Their dogs still in harness. I had a bit to eat and a cup of tea, and was hitching up my team of dogs when they left for the scene of the kill. Arriving there, my moose was already half-skinned and we finished it, loaded up, and went back.

Next morning we started off, breaking trail all day and cutting. We came back after it was dark. We did the same the next day. Third day, we loaded up our toboggans and drove up to the end of the broken trail.

We made our camp here and every day we pushed our line

farther ahead. This was the year dogs had sickness and some of our dogs fell sick. We had two teams among the four of us. I had two sick dogs in my team of four. I had raised pups which were a year old then. I had been breaking them in for harness work, they did all right, and I was thinking that a little more training would do the trick. Back home we had more sick dogs when we left. Two nights later, I had only two dogs left, old ones. Early in the morning they could be off in a flash, but later on in the day they got played out and I had to get a pole and push from the back with this pole.

We were going deep into the hills to trap marten, but we had to turn back. This was our third unsuccessful attempt too. First time on account of shortage of food after going nearly halfway. Our second try was the same, but this one was on account of the weather. For more than a week, the chinook wind blew and took all the snow away. Still we kept going till we hit a big creek, which had broken up and was full of water. This had happened in midwinter and made us turn back. I guess some of the oldtimers remember it too.

Things were not so good for the rest of the season that year. Dogs are used for travelling in wintertime and something like this hits in midwinter, makes things that much harder for us. We raised dogs after that, but not as good and I think those were the last of the good sleigh dogs. Back home all the sick dogs had died. Dogs were good travellers before this and I once made thirty-two miles in three hours from Simpson to Two Islands. Halfway I turned one of my dogs loose and let him go ahead. This produced some kind of chain reaction that lasted till I got to Two Islands. I ran most of the way myself too, but I was younger then and had lots of kick in me.

Later on we learned that other trappers lost their dogs too. One old fellow at Burned Island lost a whole team of seven dogs. Yes, I had left home with four good dogs and got back with two. Later on, on the visit to the traps on this same line, there were wolves and they ate up the dead dogs. Maybe some of *them* died with the sickness.

Next time, I will tell you about something more pleasant than this as I want to take you deep into the mountains. By now you should have overcome your fear of high places too, so I will do that!

13 Setting Traps for Marten

Our fall catch of fish was up on a stage, and trapping season was just around the corner when Dad suggested that we go into the hills for marten. Dad had been there before in his younger days and knew the back hill country, back of Sibbeston Lake. So everything had to be done according to his book, while us boys were still green, still in the learning stage of this game. It does not take one day or one trip on a trapline to learn everything about it, but the knowledge is accumulated down through the years.

First the preparations. Wood to be cut and we cut and hauled it in to our winter camp, where our mother and sisters were going to stay. Toboggans and dog harness for two teams had to be made to fit for the trip. Mountain country is pretty rugged and sharp rocks will carve the toboggan thin in no time. Snowshoes, axes, rifles and shells, all the tools of the trade. Everyone busy for a week, mother and sisters looking after the mitts and moccasin angle. And, finally, the big day.

We had to break trail from the start and it took us three days

to go through the big, rough candy mountain, through a pass. West of this candy mountain, which is nothing but rocks, the hills are all tree covered. Hills, spruce and jackpine country, good for marten. Some very high hills have bald tops. From hilltops the country is nice to look at, but you try to go somewhere and you go up and down, up and down. What seems only a few miles takes two days sometimes. One bad hill took us four hours to climb. So steep we had to rest the dogs every so often. Coming back we had to put dog chains under the toboggans to hold them back some, and coming down took about half an hour.

After getting into the wooded hills, we started setting traps for marten. Steel traps at first, till we ran out of them. Then we started to make traps on the spot, called deadfalls. They are made all of wood, except for the bait, which is meat or anything the marten will take and eat. Anyway, every night around the campfire, everyone could be busy making bait sticks for the next day. Ten for each man and there were four of us. Every night the same till we turned back. This kind of trap takes quite some time to make and set. First the bottom log, which is cut three feet long and should be four inches thick. Next, the top one, four inches too, but this one is a whole tree. The bottom log lies between two standing trees and the top one sits and rests on it. The big end of the top log is the business end, and care is taken to see that top and bottom fit nicely together. Next comes the pen. This is cut from logs three inches thick and over a foot long. About a dozen is plenty and these are pushed and planted into a U-shaped pen. The pen is about two feet from the business end of the top log. Now comes more logs over the top one, these are long ones and their only job is to add weight. The top log is now lifted to test the weight, which should be in the neighbourhood of forty pounds.

Our bait stick is a little piece of knife-planed wood, about nine inches in length and a quarter inch thick. The baited end is pointed to go through the bait. The next item is also a little piece of wood, a quarter inch thick, four inches long and round. Green willows are considered ideal for this. I might call this a trigger. It is the one piece that trips the set and makes the weight drop on the animal.

Now the weighted top log is lifted, the stick holding the bait goes under it over the bottom one, the piece that I call trigger is put in a standing position on top of the bait stick at the empty end, which is over the bottom log. The trigger will stand upright under the forty-pound weight, and the opening of the pen is closed at the top with spruce boughs, which are laid on top. The trap is now set and can be covered with more spruce boughs.

Our grandfathers have used this type of set for different animals, bear included. The size and weight vary according to the size of the animal it is intended for. I have caught wolverines in this kind of set, not marten sets but wolverine sets. The weight is very important and should kill the animal outright, no struggling in the trap. When rabbits are plentiful, they get caught in the set too, whisky-jacks, ravens, and I have seen chickens get caught in them too.

On a long trip like this our grub and dog feed pile gets pretty low at times. One place, Fred and I shot two moose. We skinned and cut up one moose and Fred filled his packsack with choice pieces of meat. We covered the meat with the hide and shovelled snow on it with our snowshoes till it was well covered. He left his packsack of meat there and we went over to the next moose only a few yards away. By the time we finished this one and I had my packsack filled too, we went back to the first one, where Fred was going to pick up his pack. When we reached it, we found it empty. A marten had entered the scene and dragged the choice meat away. We did not have an axe with us and we did not set a trap for the marten.

Farther on, I went hunting one day and ran into a herd of caribou and I shot four, all in a day's work. Here we made a stage for the meat and put it up on this stage. We had a big camp nearby and by the light of the campfire we feasted away on roasted ribs and heads. We also smashed every leg bone to get the marrow, which is something like candy to us on the trapline.

Days later we turned back, travelling by day and camping when night came. By and by we got back to Sibbeston Lake and home. We have been away from home for a good thirty-two days. Next trip only us boys went and every morning we skinned marten. The marten is a clean animal, no strong odour about him like the mink, which some people don't like. We take frozen marten in our blankets when we go to bed at night. Next morning they can be thawed out and we skin them, discard the carcasses. When we reached home we could count our catch, eighty-five pelts, mostly marten.

This was the final trip and we never have been in there again after that, more than twenty years ago now. Maybe some young ambitious trapper could go in there and make a big killing. The quality of the pelt may not count, but quantity would, I'm sure. Of course, I am not saying that anyone could go in there and make a fortune. Maybe it sounds that way, but a person has to have some know-how about the bush, or it will be a big mistake. There are no rabbits, but lots of chickens and ptarmigans. Even high up on hills we find lakes, some are good-sized ones, and beaver houses too. Little creeks run out from these lakes and there are fish in them too. These streams run year round and we had to build bridges to cross some of them. Most big hills have divides, where creeks run in opposite directions. Down in the low valleys, it's bitingly cold and seems to penetrate right to the very bone. Up on high places, it's nice and mild, the trees are almost soft. We generally camp on high hills to get away from the cold. The marten also gets away from the cold by travelling along high ridges and we set most of our traps in high places too.

14
Spring Migration

April is the month of the geese to the bushman. It means the month the geese migrate north. The moon of the geese in Slavey. This is the nearest moon to Easter, or the day the sun dances. If you are an observing kind, you will notice that birds, small ones, appear around the last quarter date on the calendar. This usually means the geese have passed north. The smaller birds ride the big ones on migration north. This is true from my personal observations. Many times I have seen a flock of geese going by my place, along the river close to shore, and noticed small summer birds come out of the flock and fly to shore and feed. So much for bird watching by the bushman.

Dog team travel is done by night in this month. It is also the last month of travel by this system. Time to put my toboggan and driving license away. Till I do, I'm like a night owl. Snow gets soupy and awful sticky by day, but it freezes to a hard crust in the cool nights. With steel runners on, a person can really go on a river. Bush trails are hard to travel this closing month. The sun melts down one side of the trail and with a load on, keeping the toboggan straight stretches one arm longer than the other, after going all night. The bushes rub your sides and slap you in the face! It's so dark on moonless nights, you can't see well, but this is only for two hours and it's day again. We usually make fire and take some refreshment, wait till it's bright enough to go. Come about nine o'clock, it's getting sticky again and time to make camp for the day. After feeding the dogs, we unroll our beddings and sleep.

I still remember my first night travel from the river to Sibbeston Lake. Dad and I had come to the river to stow away our winter gear and now we were going back by night. An hour away from the river we saw fresh moose tracks and every dog went after it. We had left our toboggan and harness at the river and the dogs had packs on, running loose. We made fire and waited

an hour till all the dogs came back, and we started off again. It was a very clear night and cold, snow frozen hard and dogs running loose all over the place. At first I took a few spills into the hard snow, dogs stepping on my snowshoes behind. Dogs are smart, so I thought I'd teach them. I took a stick and every time I heard one close to my heel, I swung the stick towards the rear. At first I hit a few of them, but learn they did, and I had to throw away my stick. Every time a rabbit hopped, every dog could be running that way too, two teams of them being loose.

Halfway to Sibbeston Lake we made fire and some tea. Here the new day came and we resumed our songless march. Nine o'clock came and we were still two hours away from home. The sun rode high up in the cloudless sky and I was getting warmer all the time and awful sleepy too. At night when it's cold, I didn't feel that sleepy, but now it was warming up and it was getting the best of me. I was ahead of Dad, going down the sunny side of a large hill, when it happened. The trail was narrow but straight in some places, and I fell asleep. I don't mean I fell, I sleepwalked on a long stretch. A guy cannot make curves in sleep and I kept going straight past the lefthand curve till I hit a tree and that woke me up. I went back to the trail and soon was sleepwalking again, to hit another tree. This happened about four times and then there was no more sleep. It was getting real good and sticky when we reached the lake and took the last and longest mile home.

I spread out my bedroll and tried to sleep after we came home. I had never slept in the daytime before and had a funny feeling trying to sleep in broad daylight. Besides, I was afraid of hitting another tree!

Trapping for winter fur ends earlier, but we still get around some, by dog team. Easter is the last time we make a trip to

town to buy our spring supplies. By this time, the fur price is way down. Mink, which leads other fur and starts the opening season at around twenty-five to thirty dollars, will bring four dollars locally now. As the goods from the store cost so high, one mink does not provide much supplies for our spring. Spring means shooting time and we always take a supply of .22 shells. If muskrats are thick, we use lots of these little shells.

Spring, to us, comes only when we see creeks open up with water. By this time, those who are going far for the spring hunt, have left home, taking a load of supplies for a month. Not much food is taken, as we live off the country most of our time. Tea, matches, tobacco, shells and maybe a little flour to make bannock. If we plan to come down the river, we take a good-sized piece of canvas and some tallow. We use tallow to waterproof our spring boats. These boats are dismantled after use and the tallow-treated canvas is put away till next spring. Paint is good too, but that same boat can't be used again, as the paint dries hard and tends to crack and break. First time I paddled down the North Nahanni in this kind of tallow-treated boat, I didn't feel safe. I could see water through the boat I was sitting in, and had the feeling it was going to come into the boat any minute. It never did and sometimes we do load them down quite a bit with our spring catch and dogs.

The boats we make could be used downstream only, lack of streamlining makes them awkward for upstream. It requires an outboard motor for that as the water is fast in most places. One year we brought a whipsaw, motor, gas, oil, hammers and nails. We made lumber with the whipsaw, planed it and built a scow. We had lots of work building the boat, but once it was made, we were okay. We went up the river, North Nahanni, as far as we could go, trailing blue smoke from the exhaust of the motor, and came back down. Our spring work was finished.

15 From Skates to Snowshoes

My three years of school at Fort Providence were not in some ways very pleasant ones if my recollections are correct. Every child, from the biggest boy down to the smallest one, was Catholic, which Freddie and I were not as yet. Many times I was teased and named "le protestant" by the other children. I was just one of them growing up and never felt any difference from any of them. At times it got too much for me to bear and one day I broke down and had to see our keeper, Sister Andruchow. She gave me a few words of consolation, ending with, "Why don't you pass them in the class, show them what you've got?" Right there I made up my mind to work hard in school and learn something. Right now, as I write this, I am still at it, and maybe someday I will go for a visit to Providence and see how the good people are doing.

I remember one time I got hit on the forehead with a hockey stick. This did not happen intentionally on the part of anybody, it was a pure accident. Everybody was out on the ice with skates when I was accidentally hit and everything went black while blue stars flew all around. The next thing I knew I was being helped up the stairs still in my ice moccasins. I slipped back into the black then, next everyone was on his knees and praying. Black again, and when I came to, I was in bed in the dormitory. I felt weak and awful shaky. Sister gave me something in a cup and I drank it. I felt something coming up, so I ran to the bathroom. Before reaching it I started vomiting and I half-staggered into the bathroom. Once relieved, I went back to my bed and soon fell asleep.

I woke next morning feeling fine, but I was told to stay in bed for a week. My meals were brought to me and I ate sitting in bed. This had happened on a Sunday. Came Sunday again and after dinner, Sister came to take my tray away. "Put your clothes on and look out the window." I did and everyone was out there, frolicking on the ice with skates. I went down the stairs, took my skates, put them on and spent the whole afternoon on skates. I was not very good on skates then, being my first year.

Learning to use a pair of snowshoes is quite similar to using a pair of skates. I felt funny when I put my first pair on, and believe me, I was pretty awkward in them. Sometimes I'd go headfirst into the snow and would get mad at my snowshoes. I figured they were just a nuisance in walking, but not now. After

years of using snowshoes every winter, I know they are there on my feet, but I never feel or notice them at all. They have become my big extra feet and I look upon them as a big help in walking, especially in deep snow. A light snowfall on good frozen ground makes walking difficult, but a good pair of snowshoes remedies that. Yes, I have used snowshoes in all kinds of country, thick bush and open muskeg, uphill and down. I was not so good at first but, by and by, I had passed the amateur mark. But I don't want to exaggerate and say that I am a full-fledged professional user of the snow feet. Some people were so good on snowshoes, they could run a moose down, but these were in the muzzle-loader days.

The first pair I made was not too good. I was the only one who could use them and I wore them out, too. My next pair was quite an improvement over the first one. Some winter evenings I spent my time making snowshoes by the light of the gas lamp. I used to break them in, bending and shaping, till I started using steam. Steam is not hard to make. All that I use is one length of stovepipe, an empty five-pound lard pail, which takes six-inch pipe very nicely, a fire and a cup of water. Half an hour in the steam bath and my snowshoes are bent and shaped without breaking. I use this system in making my toboggans too.

Some people make snowshoes out of spruce, which they claim is much lighter than the birch. Maybe it is, but I know it breaks easy, while the birch will stand a lot of abuse. Camping under the stars on the bush trails in deep snow, the snowshoes are used as shovels to scoop out the snow to the ground, where beds are made for the night. I have used them for taking ice chips out of the holes I chisel through the ice when setting beaver traps.

Snowshoes can be made in different shapes and sizes. My standard bushtrail size is three feet long and eight inches at the widest. I have a pair that I use in March and it's close to five feet long and about a foot wide. These are not good on the bush trails, but off the trail they are. With other things, care makes them go a long way, and it is the same with the snowshoes.

When I make a pair of snowshoes, I lace them with babiche, the front part, the rear part, and the midsection where the feet go. This midsection lacing wears out first and has to be repaired once or twice a winter, depending on the amount of use. It also depends on the quality of the babiche used in lacing. This, in turn, depends on the age of the hide-bearer. The older the moose or caribou, the tougher the hide. Making babiche is considered women's work, but I have tried my hand at it and have turned out some pretty good babiche.

Well, this and other pieces I have written about my winter wonderland have been my treasured memories of bygone years, which I have come to share with you. Memories that time alone shall not erase from my mind.

16 Observation and Experience

May is the month of sounds of all kinds. Sounds of wings, honking geese, calls of mating birds of every kind and the sound of running waters as rivers wake up from their long winter sleep. Old Muddy, the Mackenzie, floats its ice and soon breaks it up and sends it down to the sea. When the river is clear of ice, it's time for boats and kickers. These two also make sounds, big sounds. To a person who has lived in the bush like me, all these sounds can be well understood. The call of the mallard is always the same, quack, quack, but the pitch of the tone can be distinguished quite clearly between a mating call and a warning of an enemy being near. This is true of birds of different kinds. No change in their language, but a change in the tone.

Rivers, too, have sounds of different pitch. A big thunderous roar means water spilling over a beaver dam. Many times I have listened for this roar along rivers on past spring hunts. On quiet evenings, the sound can be heard many miles away. Beaver sometimes build a dozen dams and the lower dam makes the biggest noise. I have never seen a beaver house with a single dam, always two or more. This helps prevent damage by the water.

Around Sibbeston Lake, where I have spent most of my time, I know every creek and lake. I have come to know the surrounding country as good as the inside of my pocket, which is empty most of the time. My pocket, not the country. As I know the country, I have no fear of getting lost. Some days I would be away all alone hunting. Comes night and I make a straight shortcut home.

In winter, with snow on the ground, trees and animal tracks can be used as a means of telling different kinds of country. Certain trees grow in certain places suited to them. A long line of big, tall spruce means a river, while the scraggy kind means muskeg. Poplars grow only on good hard ground. All these observations I have put to good use when hunting alone. My close observation of animals, too, comes in handy sometimes. The amphibious mink will travel along rivers, while the rambling marten prefers hills and high country. Caribou will travel on frozen muskeg in light snow, but as the snow gets deep it will retire to some hillside.

All this and many more I have learned the hard way. It took years to accumulate all this knowledge about the bush life. Big things and little things. Camping for one. I remember the first time I went alone on the trapline. During the first day out everything went fine and I never felt alone. But came night and I built my camp, my fire. Slowly the daylight vanished to the west and a feeling of being alone, surrounded by black night, gripped me. I had my dogs tied near and all around, but that didn't help. I did not have a watch to tell time, but I kept the fire going till I really got sleepy. I tried to stay awake, but sleep got stronger. I was thinking I could lie in my eiderdown and watch, so I crawled in it.

I woke next morning in full daylight, everything just as it had been last night. I had a good laugh that morning and nearly choked on a piece of bannock during breakfast. My next night wasn't that bad, but that first one was quite an experience for me. Things like that can have a bad psychological effect on a first-timer. They may make a person do the wrong thing, but keeping busy is the one and only cure and I strongly recommend that. Be always willing to learn and be always on the move, a going concern. It takes training and years to build character, and I guess my ancestral traits were strong too.

I always have a feeling that the bush man and his white brother have lots of things in common, and we have certain things we could learn from each other, people being interesting subjects too. You know, things that we could put to good use, provided that we apply them right. This and other forces have compelled me to write a few pages when I have the time and I hope you like it also.

17 Fishing Time

Some people think and say that life on the trapline far away from the city lights must be awfully dull, monotonous. Others say that trapping is a lazy man's occupation. Life in the bush is mighty different from one under the city lights, but it's not dull as you think. Maybe I don't see a hockey game or a picture show every night, but I think life can be well filled and every minute of it too. Life anywhere can be dull if you make it that way.

Trapping, like any other occupation, is hard work. We have to cut a lot of trees every year and when snow gets deep, we work the hardest. This in cold weather too. You have to eat well and be stout-hearted to face the north wind. This is far from a lazy man's occupation and is not a career for those who are on diets. In the summertime we don't trap and since that's the only time we see people and people see us doing what comes naturally, they think we're lazy.

Summertime is fishing time and is a test of patience sometimes. We do not fish for sport, as some people do. We do it because we don't want to go to bed hungry. Some white people from outside think our fish are too small, but these people are used to seeing "Moby Dick" anyway!

Some of our fishes spawn in the spring, while other kinds spawn in the fall. When the creeks are open and free of ice and other obstacles, spawning fish go upstream as far as they can. On their way in, a net will catch them quite easily, but on the way out, they are hard to catch with a net. Literally millions are born every year, but fish are great cannibals and feed on their young. In the summer you see boats of every description, and nearly every one of these boats has a pole sticking up from it. Don't look for a flag because this is just a fishing rod. Some are expensive rods, but I don't think it changes the luck. Mine is usually a young poplar, cut and the bark peeled off while green. This is heavy when green, but when dried it's the lightest wood that I know. With this, I could fish with one hand and shoo flies and mosquitoes with the other.

Fish traps were used in the days of our grandfathers and I have seen them in my early days. These traps are made to catch the fish as they come down creeks after spawning. The creek is dammed, with a spillway down a chute. A low stage or fish container is built just below the spilling water. Fish coming down will go down the chute and drop into the trap container. When the water is deep, fish come down in the daytime. When the water is shallow, they stay in the heavy pools and come down only at night. Only certain kinds go up to spawn, but other kinds join in also. Some fish spend the summer inland and will come down only when the water is getting too shallow.

One fall in September, at a creek near my home, I built a makeshift trap for fish. The water was low, about four inches deep. I did not work hard and had my trap set and went home.

Next morning I went back, carrying a sack to put the fish in. Reaching my trap I took out all the fish from the container into the sack. I also counted my one night's catch and had seventy-three fish. All blue fish (grayling). The third day, I had to take my trap out of the water, as something else turned up.

Along the rivers, fish don't spawn in the fall, but in lakes the white fish do. At Sibbeston Lake, where we used to stay, we catch white fish in nets at the lake outlet. This spot remains open all winter and some years ducks winter there, feeding on fish eggs. This outlet is shallow in the fall and you could step in and take out your supper with your hand. First time we went there to fish, I couldn't sleep, (fish are noisy when there are plenty in one little spot like this, I learned later). Birds and land animals such as bear, foxes, lynx and wolves feed on the spawning fish in shallow water, but the fish do not leave the spawning ground. Later on in October, when a big storm comes, it pushes the water to the south end. When this tide goes out, the fish will go. This storm is usually the turning point to winter and the lake begins to freeze over. Sometimes sheer weight in number will break a net or two in half.

Netfishing under the ice is cold work for the hands, especially when there is a wind blowing from the North. But fresh-caught fish is good. Our fall-caught fish is mainly for the dogs. One year,

Father Feuvrier fished under ice. He came to the lake on a Friday and on Saturday I came home after being away for a week. He came to see us after I came home and said he wanted to put out his nets before Sunday. So I went with him and by the light of the moon, we ran two nets under the ice for him. After we finished the setting, we sat in the shack, talking. I explained everything about fishing under the ice to him. After I finished my lecture, a faraway look came into his eyes and he said to me; "Dear boy, you can repeat what you just said about a hundred times and still I won't know." I knew right then that he couldn't catch his quota for a plane load, as he had planned. For about two weeks poor Father Feuvrier fished, but the fish avoided his nets and the weather turned bitterly cold. Finally, he had to come home to Simpson, leaving his tangled nets to us. My brother Fred fished and put up the required amount of fish for him. Later that winter, the Mission sent a plane to pick up the fish.

Sibbeston Lake is not known for fishing under the ice with a line and hook, and we never tried that. Other surrounding lakes have trout but none in Sibbeston Lake.

We fished with line and hooks one year on Little Doctor Lake and caught some pretty nice fish, including trout. Some of these trout are big to us, but you have to see it to believe it. This lake goes through the rock candy mountain and has walls of rock on two sides. It is also very deep and partner, that's only putting it mildly.

18
Gun and Axe

December is the month of short days and long cold nights on the trapline. It is also my birth month and I am forty-four years old. Unlike some people, who are reluctant to admit their true age, I am proud of mine. Though life is hard and my financial state of affairs is not always good, the best things in life are free anyway. It is only the crazy white man that piles up money, not knowing that he can't take it with him. Money brings fame and recognition to some lucky people. Some rich people use their money to help the less fortunate. There is more to it than that, but I don't want to offend anybody. To others it has brought ruin and corruption. Even the good things of life have their evils too, if used well but not wisely.

Guns and the axe are two of the dangerous tools of my trade, and I remember one winter day not too long ago, when I had a near-accident. I had been tracking some caribou all day and shot one just before nightfall. I skinned and covered my kill and headed back to my camp where I had my dogs. It was dark when I arrived, but I hitched up my dogs and went back to the scene of my kill. Near the scene, I cut enough dry wood for the fire and had to cut some green trees to use the boughs for my bed in the snow. I took a hard blow with my axe at the first tree. My axe glanced right off the frozen tree and went towards my leg. With all the muscles put behind it, I could not stop it. Call it intuition or sixth sense but something told me to move my leg out of there fast and I did. The axe caught and gripped my pant leg, but luckily I did not get a nick or scratch. I had moved my leg just in time, but this was too close for comfort and even talking about it now gives me the cold chills. A dull axe does that, but a sharp one stays with the wood.

Careful as we are, accidents do happen sometimes. One year us three brothers were alone on a spring hunt and Henry cut his foot. We happened to be all at camp that day and I was doing some chores around the fire when I heard a yell of pain that sounded like Henry, so I went over there. Fred was already there and Henry was holding his foot, blood all over the place, on trees, moss, axe and his clothes. The whole blade had cut into the bone from the inside, where all the veins and muscles go, and blood was coming out by the gallons. We wrapped his foot and took him to camp. We had first-aid kits, but the bandages were good only for little knife cuts, so we cut all our spare shirts and towels, used them for bandages. We washed and used them again. Blood kept coming out and we couldn't stop it. I have heard of tourniquets applied to injured limbs, but I have never witnessed an actual application and had doubts about its use. Finally, we dressed up the foot and put it in a large moccasin. Blood still came, but slowly it dried into the moccasin and this sealed it good enough to stop the blood.

After two days we soaked the foot in water and carefully

removed the bloodied moccasin and dressing. Long strings of clotted blood hung from the cut, but no fresh blood. We dressed it up in dry cloths and once the bad bleeding stopped, Henry took it more quietly. For a week he couldn't sleep. Suffering from pain, loss of sleep and blood, he started saying funny things. Fred and I looked at him with a new concern, but Henry slept well that night and our concern soon vanished. One man had to be at camp with him while the other went hunting. We had to hunt for our food, but luckily we were close to a lake with fish in it and lots of ducks.

Fred and I worked every day and soon we had two boats. We put all our hunting gear into the boats and every day we drifted down. Henry was helped in and out of boats. For one full month he went on hands and knees, and by the time he walked, we were in Simpson. This was back in the fifteen beaver days and we didn't have too much trouble getting forty-five beavers for the three of us. Beaver was plentiful in that part of the country too.

Guns and axes are "musts" on the traplines and are safe if handled properly. My grandfather was cleaning his shooting iron when it accidentally discharged and he had part of his hand blown away. I was just a child then and my recollections are pretty dim, but I remember that we had to go to town for medical aid for grandfather. He didn't know that the old muzzleloader was loaded, and had one hand at the end.

19 Entertainment on the Trapline

All the winter months on the trapline seem short because the days are short, especially December. March is the only month that stretches from winter to spring, and that makes it a rather long month in the North. A trapper does not rush or get up early in the morning to reach a certain destination in March. He is usually awake before sunrise, but he lies in his warm eiderdown and gets up only just before the sun comes up. He knows that he can't have breakfast in bed and has to get up to make his fire anyway. This is primarily to watch the sunrise, which is a beauty to behold sometimes. Vivid colours of pinkish reds and flamelike orange are quite a sight to see. Beautiful sunrises and crashing sunsets, but sometimes they are warnings of approaching storms. Sometimes the colours are not there at all, but a long shaft of sunlight shoots up from the sun into the sky. This usually means a very windy day, but no snowfall or rain if it is summer.

Many times I have been up, had breakfast and sat by my campfire just to see the sunrise and find out the weather picture.

I generally wait till the sun warms things up a bit before I hitch my team up for the day. I know that the toboggan glides over the snow easier in March than December, January and February. Down slopes, I'd be riding, and sometimes singing and yodelling, with the trees and chickadees for an audience that don't applaude me any. Uphills, my singing stops and I'd be walking and mushing from the rear. The sound of a whip or a breaking stick spurs the dog team onward to the hilltop and then, ride again. Sometimes I work hard and really earn my keep, often for nothing, but other times I am bringing a payload home. I usually sing when I have a payload.

March, 1963, according to my diary, I had finished trapping winter fur and prepared to go beaver trapping before Easter. I loaded up the toboggan with my grub and Number Four traps, and headed in the direction of Sibbeston Lake, to a creek that I knew. After going for three hours, I hit a "cat" road, which went west in my direction, so I followed it. At the creek, I stopped and tied my dogs. I took my gun and big snowshoes, went up the creek, looking for beaver lodges. I found one, so I came back for some traps and that same day, I had traps set for beaver. Next day, I followed the "cat" road some more, making side trips and setting more traps as I did. After travelling and working all day, I made my camp by the roadside. There was lots of busted dry wood and I went up and down the road and collected my woodpile for the night. So far I didn't see anybody, and I just sat there alone with absence to make the heart grow fonder. An oil company was doing some seismic work in that particular region that winter and made a wide road. At eight o'clock I began to hear a distant throb of a labouring diesel engine and saw headlights lighting up the road. Nearer and nearer it came and soon I felt my trapping ground shaking under me as the tractor came by and stopped. A bearded man stepped off and greeted me by the light of the campfire. We made friends right there and sat for over an hour chewing the fat.

A week later, I went to see my beaver traps and as I came down the road I drove into a camp. Minding my own business, I drove past and kept going. I had traps near my old camp a mile further on, and I was going to camp there anyway. To my surprise, there was a camp there also, but I had to stop and I did. Invited, I had supper with the gang and was asked an avalanche of questions. I cooked my dogfeed over an open fire and fed my dogs for the night. Then I went back to visit with the men. Soon, Bill Singletary, the boss, came to announce that there would be a show at eight. I was invited to the movie too, so I went and saw Audrey Hepburn in *Breakfast at Tiffany's.* During intermissions, a lot of wisecracking went back and forth among the side-burned oilmen and I nearly split my sides with laughter. The picture was a comedy-type show too, and that made me forget my beaver traps for a while.

Up until then, I had never dreamed that I'd see a picture show like this right on my trapline, but I guess I did. I made one more trip to the traps after this, and then it was time to go into town for Easter.

20 Tribute to the Oldtimers

Learning to identify animals from the tracks left in the snow is one of the first lessons that a young trapper learns if he is to take care of himself in the bush. Lessons that are sometimes learned by bitter experiences that leave indelible marks on a man and stay with him till his number comes up. Even a skillful hunter does not always bring meat home. Often the tide turns in favour of the hunted. There is a difference between moose and caribou tracks, though to a newcomer, they appear to be the same. Moose takes longer steps, while caribou tends to drag his hooves in the snow between tracks. But the first lesson is to find out which way it has gone. This is done by poking the ends of oblong tracks with the rifle stock. One end will be soft and the other will be hard. The hard end points in the right direction. Next is to find out how old the track is. This is also done by poking the tracks, which might be frozen and hard. This means it's old, while a soft one indicates freshness.

Though I'm not much of a good hunter, I had to learn all the

lessons of the bush. There may be other ways to make a living, but the white man's way of life does not always prove ideal or satisfactory to me yet. Change takes time and a melting pot they tell us. In my younger days I have seen many a good hunter track down a moose, both summer and winter. Outstanding among them was Joseph Cli. Not knowing much of the white man's language and ways, he followed the traditions of our tribe, and has fed many a hungry mouth. He, being reared in an atmosphere of nomadic existence, possessed all the cunning skill of a real bushman.

In winter when a storm rages at its highest, he is gone before dawn. This is because he knows that the howl of the wind kills all other sounds and he has a better chance to stalk a moose. Very late in the evening, he comes back into his house, snow adhering to his clothes. If he gets a moose, and lots of times he did, he will be staying home tomorrow and all owners of dog teams will be going to the scene of the kill to bring back the meat. The meat will be distributed and shared by all in a village. The hide is also brought home and is usually given to the family that gets the backbone. Sometimes the choice parts are cooked and a feast is proclaimed. Everyone has a holiday then.

Tracking a moose in summertime is different from in winter, but Cli and other oldtimers knew how it's done. Uncle Cli knows certain places frequented by moose and these places are frequented by him too. There are also places where there is salt and moose will go there to lick the salts. Meat-hauling bush trails usually lead away from these places too, trails that are now grown over from lack of use. These trails were used till the game regulations were changed and we were allowed to kill one bull moose in September. They have now been changed again, but nobody uses the trails. So, the feeling is that an era has ended there and a new one taken hold. Uncle Cli knows that something is happening too, but he says he is not young any more and prefers to retire into the sidelight. Being an old veteran of the bush, Cli had some pretty close calls with nature. According to him, one time following a moose on a mountainside, a snow avalanche nearly claimed him. He was young then and had the agility of a cat, which helped him to save himself, losing only his rifle in the process.

In his prime, summer days were mostly spent away from home in the bush. Sometimes he got caught in summer storms and came home wet. Other times he couldn't come home in a little canoe on account of the storm, and camped by himself. Some of these storms can really put up whitecaps too.

It is oldtimers like these men, Joseph Cli, George Sibbeston, and others, who had a hand in giving me all the medicine (know-how) of the bush life. This medicine is something that money can't buy, but it can be put to good use, coupled with one's own experiences. These aged people, which of course includes my dad, had altruistic reasons for doing and saying certain things and I have the same reasons for bringing it to you. It can't be said that a good man did or said something because we all have faults, our weaknesses. Everyone has dreams of Utopia, but being humans, we cannot achieve absolute perfection. Impossible, but the idea is to stimulate thinking and avoid some of the unnecessary hardships and sufferings. Sometimes people see and realize things only when it's too late, but we can't all be in the same boat and surely some of the younger people could make use of what they see and hear. These are things that our younger folks should keep and practice till their campfires are dimmed and the tribal drums are stilled.

21 Making Things out of Wood

Our tribal folklore has many stories of old, old times, and according to these stories, I think we have been here a long, long time too. Some of the stories tell of big clumsy monsters that were flesh-eating mammals. These huge beasts roamed the land and frequently fed on people. All these monsters are said to be driven underground and some were slaughtered by two young men destined to do that. Other stories deal with the evolution that brought the animals to their present state as we know them today. Our stories about this period differ from those of the white man. He uses what he calls the scientific method and we use the "eye and ear" system. We tell stories of what we see and hear, and all the stories have been handed down from one generation to another by word of mouth down through the ages.

Some of our oldtimers are fabulous storytellers, but most of them are reluctant to tell stories. It's hard to get them in a talking mood, but when an opportunity presents itself, then they do tell stories. Some tell adventure stories while others tell about the wild bush man that doesn't seem to exist. It makes them afraid to go into the bush in the summertime. Up to now, I have never seen anything that resembles a wild bush man and I've kept my eyes peeled for that. Only once, on a spring hunt, did I hear a shot fired near me. I saw ducks fly away from the danger zone, so I fired my gun too, as a signal, and went there to look. I looked all around but nobody, so I built a fire and made lots of smoke. Still nobody came and I figured it must be someone trespassing on our territory. I don't aim to scare you away, so I think I will change our subject.

I have a craving for making things out of wood and I've made toboggans, snowshoes, boats, violins and guitars. I have also made gunstocks if a broken one is handed to me. The hardest wooden thing to make is the violin. It takes so much time, patience and skill. The neck piece requires hardening and it takes time and know-how. First, I make a roughly hewn neck and keep it in a tub of water. It floats at first, but it becomes waterlogged and sinks like a stone after being in water for a long period. It stays in there till I get the required heftiness I want. I take it out then, let it dry enough so the glue will stick good and apply a good thick coat of Ambroid cement. This seals it up in a caselike enclosure and no air is permitted to enter. The sealed neck is put to dry away from the sun. This coat of Ambroid cement prevents wood from cracking in drying. After it's dry, the coating is removed and four holes are bored through, two from each side. These are for the pegs used in tuning the instrument when finished. I use a homemade hand-turning drill and a lot of time is spent doing it. If not, I break it and have to start all over again.

Using the bored holes as guides, I run a round tapered steel rod, which is red hot and burns its way through, increasing the hole size to accommodate the pegs. Later on, I smooth the insides with a tapered round file and this takes away the burned parts. There is some shrinkage that occurs in drying, but I usually make the parts oversize because sanding also makes it smaller. This neck piece when finished is a piece of good hard wood and has to be, to take the strain of four steel strings.

The sides are planed thin and shaped on forms to dry. These come in four pieces and I make them of birch. These do not require hardening. When the sides are dry and retain their formed shape, they are glued carefully together. The next hardest part to make is the top, which is spruce and free from knots and blemish. The F sound holes are cut out in slanted angles and have to be correct. The top and bottom are carved out on the insides while green and it is thin. These two parts can be glued

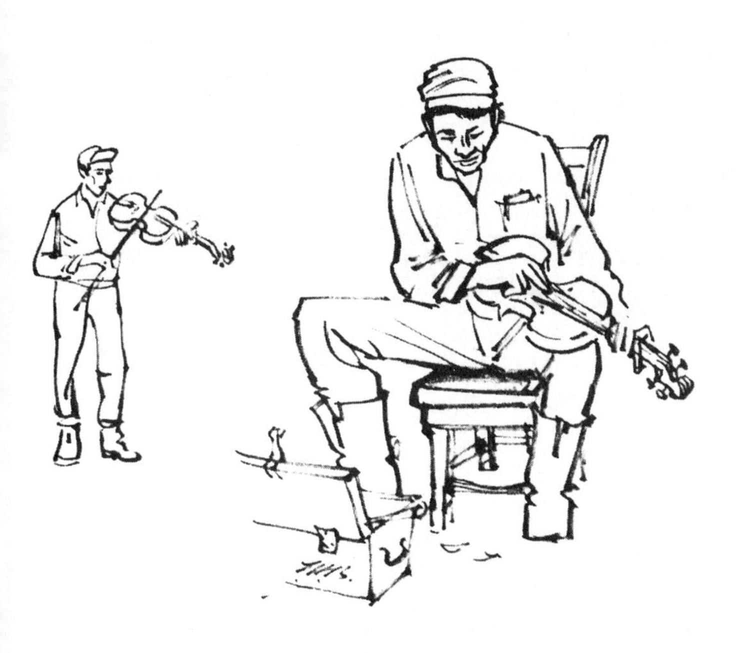

to the sides in their green state after getting the sound post in place. The edges are trimmed off after the glue sets. The top and bottom have to be glued at the same time if green. If not, shrinkage will take place and misshape the sides. The neck is glued after careful fitting because it has to be straight and at an angle. Strain is avoided for forty-eight hours to set the glue. After that, I can test my violin for sound. I can't play it, but I know I can make it.

All this requires patience and skill because I don't use any special tools. All I use are my axe, knife and a few homemade tools. My only big problem is the finish, I can't varnish it the way it's done at the factory, but I guess I will learn some day.

22
Emergency Trip

To be on the trapline means a lot of things, big and small. Tight-fitting clothes are usually frowned on, as they interfere with movement. The moosehide thongs that secure the feet to the snowshoes are something that has to be watched. They are adjustable but if adjusted too tight on the feet, can produce blisters on the toes. Even a tiny blister can get infected and become a major problem. Certain blood types in people make them very easily infected. Others seem to fare better. Being many miles away from civilization, with no means of communications and transportation always a problem, a person has to be alert and watch for things like that. Of course sickness, which has no respect for rank or nobility, sometimes does strike.

One fall I went up to the fishery on the Slave Lake with the Cli brothers in their fish scow. We fished until the scow had its load and left. Past and below Fort Providence, travelling by night, we hit a rock and broke through the bottom of the scow in three places. We unloaded the fish and took the boat out of the water. We had some spare planks and used them to repair our boat. We reloaded the fish in the scow and travelled only by day to get home with our load. At Two Islands we unloaded and pulled the scow up from the river. I was allotted a hundred sticks of fish, which I hung up on a stage. After helping the Cli boys with their boat, I was going to go to Sibbeston Lake, where my folks were. We usually live there most of the time and James Horesay , an uncle, stays there with us too. It takes us three days by pack to reach the lake in September just before the fish come to spawn. We put up enough fish for the winter and trap all winter there. Comes June, just before the mosquitoes come out, we'd be pulling out of there to spend the summer along the big, wide Mackenzie.

Fred and Henry had come and helped us some, pulling up the boat. After we finished the boat, I left for the lake with my brothers, arriving there two days later. It was getting cold, with a light snow already on the ground, and lakes were starting to freeze over. My folks were at our winter camp, but Uncle Jim was still fishing at the northern end of the lake. The lake had frozen over hard and glass smooth, so I put on a pair of skates and went down to see Uncle Jim. I have known Uncle since I came back from school, but on this visit he looked different to me. I left soon because I had to be home before dark and I was wondering why Uncle looked the way he did. Maybe it was because I had been away on a long trip and had just arrived back. Little did I know that Uncle Jim was going to pass away that same winter, but he didn't look sick at all then.

Came time to set traps, so us boys went into the hills, coming back after a few days with a load of caribou meat. While we were away, Uncle, Aunt and an adopted child had come to stay with us at the house that they had nearby. He had fishnets under the ice where they stayed and every two days, he went to see his nets, bringing home the catch. He also went to set a few traps up the creek, but did not stay away from home as long as he used to. He came back after three days. We were busy every day, as this is usually so at the start of the season.

November came and went fast and soon it was December. Uncle Jim started to complain of headaches. We thought it would be just an ordinary headache and would go away after a while. But he did not appear to be improving any and some days he couldn't eat. Concerned about uncle's condition, our dad sent Freddie and Henry to Two Islands along the Mackenzie river, where Joseph Cli and some of our relations live. They made a forced trip all the way and back, Cli himself and our older brother, Jimmy, with them. Joseph Cli, another uncle, was Indian chief then. He said the sick man must be taken to a doctor in Simpson. After the dogs had a brief rest of one day for the long, cold trip, we got ready to go. Our Two Islands relatives were going home too, and that made it quite a gang, with five dog teams in all.

I did not know who was taking Uncle Jim in his sleigh for the trip. We were up very early that morning and were to be underway at five o'clock. At breakfast Uncle Cli turned to me and told me that I was to take the sick man. I felt that it should be done by some older person, and this was quite a thing that fell into my lap. Being young with absolutely no experience in this kind of work, I had to think twice before I said, "Yes I will do that." All my dog feed for the trip was to be carried for me in other sleighs and I was going to take sick Uncle only. I had to ride so the sleigh with Uncle inside could be controlled, dogs are usually wild on first take-off.

It was very dark when I pulled my sleigh in front of Uncle

Jim's house and went inside. We picked him up in his blankets and carried him out into my sleigh. He had been sick for quite some time now, and to me he appeared to be sleeping hard. That's what I thought anyway. I got my brother Jimmy aside and told him that. He told me that Uncle was sick in the head and was in a coma. I knew then that Uncle had a poor chance to live and I must try my best to hurry him in.

At the start I couldn't see good but after a while, my eyes could pick out trees good even in the dark as we bounded along the narrow trail. Away from Sibbeston Lake and up the hill we went. There were two teams ahead of me and two in the back. It was bright and cold when we reached the hilltop and our caravan headed downhill, racing against time. I got pretty cold standing still while riding, so once in a while I ran where the trail was good in some places. Downhill now I had to ride, as the sleigh swings wide and off the trail. I knelt in the back and did two things at one time. I controlled my team and prayed, asking the Boss to give me time to finish my job that I was told to do. Uncle Jim lay very still all the time and only once he brushed the blanket aside and asked me where we were and what wind was blowing. He slipped back into sleep-like coma and to me, he was just sleeping after many sleepless nights of suffering. This also was my first close contact with a very sick person. Close enough to be an uncle too.

It was dark again when I pulled my sleigh in front of the doorway leading into Chief Cli's house and carried Uncle in. After feeding our dogs, we travelers went to bed early while the women and others kept watch through the night. They also changed Uncle into dry clothes for the day's journey next morning. We were halfway to Simpson from here, about thirty-two miles. It was along the river, just on the edge of the rough,

piled-up ice. Shelf ice along the shore is generally smooth and ideal for toboggan travel till January. Preparations were made early, and in the dark we hitched up our teams and I had someone to help me with mine till I got on the river. I straightened my dogs, I had six on this particular journey, and was underway for Simpson. In the dark, I knelt in the back of the toboggan and did the two things I had been doing since yesterday. I did not want Uncle to pass away before I brought him in. He lay there in the toboggan just ahead of me, very still, and there were lots of things that went through my head since we left Sibbeston Lake.

We did not stop to make tea and it was already dusk when we pulled into town and nosed our teams for Bud Alley's bunkhouse. I had just a brief pause at the bunkhouse, and mushed on to the hospital. I halted at the doorway and went inside. Father Joseph Turcotte was in charge of the Mission at the time and happened to meet me. Father and I went to carry Uncle Jim inside on a stretcher. We brought Uncle into a room and were surprised to see Aunt come in. There had been a plane to the lake after we left and she came on the plane. I breathed a sigh of relief now that Uncle was in the hospital. I had to tend to my dogs so I left for the bunkhouse.

Next day I visited at the hospital and went to the store to buy things to take home with me. The plane had taken all the heavy stuff like flour and sugar, so my load was not going to be big. I visited again and Uncle Jim was alive, though in a coma when I left for home about noon. My travelling companions and I had spent two days in town by then. We stopped overnight at Cli's house, and next day there were only two teams going to Sibbeston Lake. My brother Freddie and I. We arrived home just before dark and went in. George Sibbeston himself happened to be there, visiting the folks. This was also the night before Christmas and we stayed up nearly all night, listening to the church services on the radio.

Later on someone brought us the sad news that Uncle Jim had passed away shortly after we left. He was originally from Fort Norman, where some relatives still live and trap. This was the first and only time that I ever made such a sad trip and I hope it stays that way always.

23
Spring on the Willow River

Spring in 1963 had come early, and I busied myself getting our little twenty-five foot scow ready for a trip down to Willow River, where some relations of mine were living. My friend and companion-to-be, George Boots, had been writing to me all winter, planning a spring beaver hunt together. Boat readied, we loaded up and pushed away from our home shores. This was thirty-two miles below Fort Simpson, N.W.T., where we have our main winter camp. Here, during the cold winter, I had trapped lynx, marten, mink and squirrels. Spring to me was another season, another way of trapping: beaver on open water. I'd spent some years spring hunting on foot, by pack. This year I was to trap and hunt by boat and kicker.

Our first day on the river was cold, as the sun hid behind the clouds. We kept going till we ran into lots of ice and high water. It turned out that the ice had neatly clogged up the wide Mackenzie. We nosed our craft into a creek and tied up for the night, sheltered from the winds. All that night we heard some

beaver splashing water with their broad paddle-like tails. We were out for beaver, I know, but it was so dark with all those clouds that I could not draw my bead on that beaver. Just when I nearly dropped back to sleep, it waked me up with another slap of its tail. I was thinking, I'll get him in the morning, but he was gone with the night.

Our beds of spruce boughs were not as comfortable as our home beds, and we were up with the dawn. We packed our things into the scow, and our four dogs, and soon were underway again, only to stop a half hour later. The river was choked up with ice; we tied up again till evening, when it broke up, and things started to move downstream once again. Night came, so we stayed there for the night. Next day we were at it again, using our 10 hp Johnson outboard motor, and drifting with the ice sometimes. In most places it was so thick it was impossible to use an outboard motor. We hit a few pieces with our boat, but we were not going full steam and it did not damage our scow.

We arrived in Willow River on the fourth day and unloaded our baggage and dogs. We visited with people and lingered long over cups of tea that day. George Boots happened to be away, and I settled down and waited two days, till he came back from a short hunt.

The third day after arrival, we packed our necessary equipment into the scow: traps, guns, shells, knives, axes, bedrolls and food. On such trips as this, we do not take much, as we will get our daily supply of food from the bush. Our chief problem is gasoline and oil for the outboard motors. My friend had one motor and I had one, and we planned to use both in places where there is fast, strong water.

We went up Willow River forty miles and camped. Next day we portaged a light canoe overland into a sluice that we knew. We paddled and circled the lake till late, shooting beaver and muskrats. We camped on the shore of this lake when it got too dark to see the gunsights. Camping on spring hunts like this, we always pick out a spot on the east side. The fading and rising twilight in the north reflects on the lakes or creeks, and this provides light just enough to shoot at anything that swims by. The wind also plays an important part in the hunt; it can and will carry the smell of a campfire smoke to the beaver's nose. A beaver has a very keen sense of smell and once it smells trouble, you have to say goodbye to that one.

Next day we skinned what beaver and muskrats we had shot the night before and packed up. We portaged our little canoe back to our scow, where we had dinner. Right after dinner we were off again, going up through Gun Rapids where the water was very strong, and we had to use the two outboards. George was at the controls and I took out my camera and snapped a picture. For the next twenty miles we set traps as we came up, and planned to remain for a few days before coming back down. We made camp and made some stretchers for our beaver hides and worked at stretching our beavers. These stretchers are usually made out of young trees, preferably spruce or tamarack, and discarded after use. This is done because we could always make them quite easily, being old hands at it. After two or three days on the stretchers, beaver hides can be rolled up or folded. Folding cracks and breaks hides, which lowers the price. Every evening we went up some distance from our camp and came floating back, always looking for beaver. Three days here and we were ready for the return trip to the mouth.

We made the downstream run in one day: about seventy miles. Some of our traps had been sprung by beavers and we reset them, planning one final trip later on. Rising or falling water plays havoc with traps in the spring. Water covers the traps and the traps will miss, often catching only a toenail off a beaver's foot. We used to joke about this, saying, "We're only toenail trappers!" But its no fun when all traps miss and you come to the end of the line with nothing to show for the day's work.

We rested for a few days at the mouth of the Willow River when we came home. Spring hunt is work mostly by night. Hunt by night when beavers come out; get a few hour's sleep, which may be interrupted and broken. Hungry bears come around sometimes, but we learn how to avoid them. The smell of food invites them, but smoke and noise keeps them away. Some guys feel safe with dogs around, as some dogs will bark at even squirrels that come around the camp. Others don't feel that way, but I have never had any trouble with bears myself. Still, I always keep my shooting iron within reach and loaded, just to be on the safe side.

Our next trip was a quick one, as the season was closing. At the end I had twenty beavers and my friend had fifteen. We saw three wolves on our way down. They appeared to be gorged full from a fresh kill nearby and were lying down in shallow

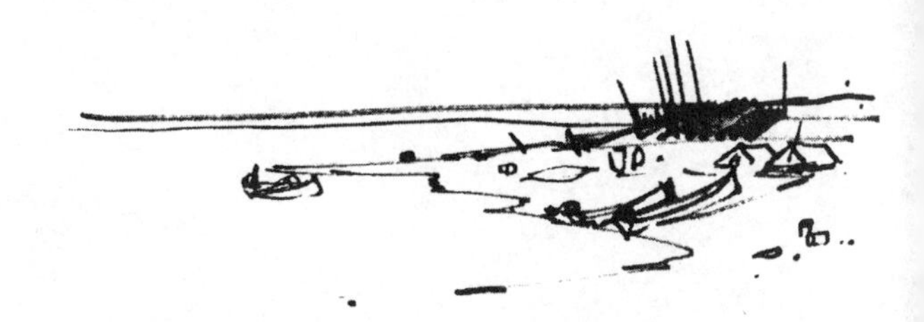

water along the river's edge. We didn't have a chance to use our guns effectively, as the water was rough at this spot.

We do not carry radios on trips we make in the spring, and it was later that we learned that nature had been rather cruel to our town, and Fort Simpson got flooded. The people were evacuated to other towns and some of our friends, especially the talky ones, sure had stories to tell us when we arrived in to sell our beavers.

Sept. 14th, 1962,
Fort Simpson, N.W.T.

Mrs. Molson;

We have come back to Simpson, and as you are interested in us people, I'm sending a copy of the August issue of the *Catholic Voice*. It has a story I wrote. I can't keep sending them, though, as we will [be] going back to the trapline soon.

Coming up from Willow River, I shot one moose. Our kids are all in school, including Florence.

We will be coming in for Xmas and New Year and hope to hear from you regarding snowshoes [etc.].

From:
John Tetso

Oct. 11/62
Fort Simpson, N.W.T.

Dear Mrs. Molson;

I just got your letter right now and I'm replying too, because we are going to go back to our trapline tomorrow if the weather permits.

There is just me and Jane home now, as the three kids are at school. Florence is in grade 1 and knows how to write her name.

Yes, you may send them little gifts if you want to. The crayons you gave them sure went great with them, especially Florence.

I think I will be able to finish your three pairs of snowshoes by December. Anyway, we are coming to town for Xmas and if it's ready, I'll send them. I will ship them collect, and you'll pay them whatever they will charge. Myself, I will take $10 for each pair.

We are really busy today, getting things to leave. Come Christmas and I write you again. Our regards.

John Tetso

December 24th, 1962,
Ft. Simpson, N.W.T.

Dear Mrs. Molson:

We came in last Friday and the gift package did arrive in good condition. Your snowshoes will be shipped after the Christmas rush. The big pair is the adult one. I made the childrens' a bit bigger, as children outgrow things. Two ways to tell which goes on which foot are these: 1. The inside frames are more straight by looking at them and the outer frames have a slightly bigger bulge, a sort of pushed-out look. 2. The knots on the moose hide thongs are always on the outside. If it's knotted on right-hand side, it goes on the right foot. These thongs will stretch when new, and have to be adjusted.

I have never been up the Nahanni where the Headless Valley is located. My trapline is 32 miles below Simpson and I trap lynx, marten, mink, beaver, muskrat, weasel, wolverine, squirrel, fox and anything that bears fur, with the exception of the rabbit. Yes, I believe you could get some animals if you want, to put on your wall. They could be prepared for that, to hang on the wall that is, for they have to be well dried to last, or they'll spoil on you.

I managed to get 20 pelts and sold 10 lynx for $130 today. Small mink is $20, beaver $15.

The Mackenzie is really rough this year, as it broke loose again 2 days after freezing over. This made it rough for travelling by dog team, but we made 32 miles in one day.

Thank you so much for the package. The kids are home with us now, as I own a house in town. They are just tickled about their presents, especially Florence.

Merry Christmas and a Happy New Year to you and family.

Sincerely,

Johnny Tetso

Dec. 27th, 1962,
Ft. Simpson, N.W.T.

Mrs. Molson,

I hope this package containing your three pairs of snowshoes arrives in good order. Please try and send us the money before we go away to the traplines. We will be here for a week after New Year's, I think, but this depends on the weather.

Thanks a lot for the gift box. This is the first time I have seen such generosity, and to tell the truth, it's the first time I have received something like this from a white person.

As you are interested in us, I will give my editor money for 1 year subscription of the *Catholic Voice*, and later on in the year I will write some animal stories for that paper. I wrote one about the snowshoes that will come shortly.

Thanking you for your correspondence and the parcel and wishing you and family a very happy New Year. May God bless you and family.

Our regards,
John Tetso

Sled "bare"

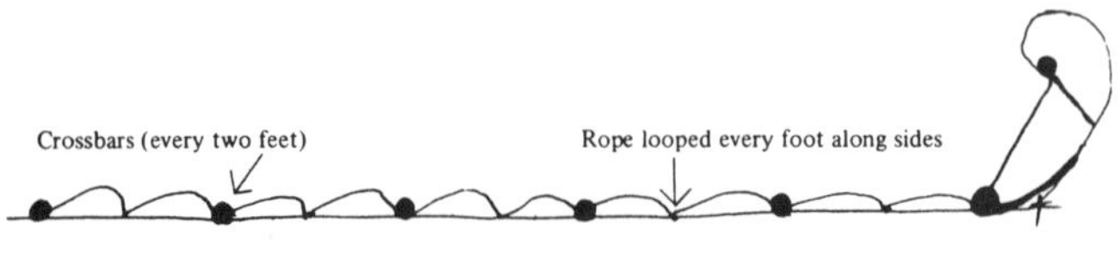

Crossbars (every two feet)

Rope looped every foot along sides

Sled loaded, with canvas wrapper and handlebars

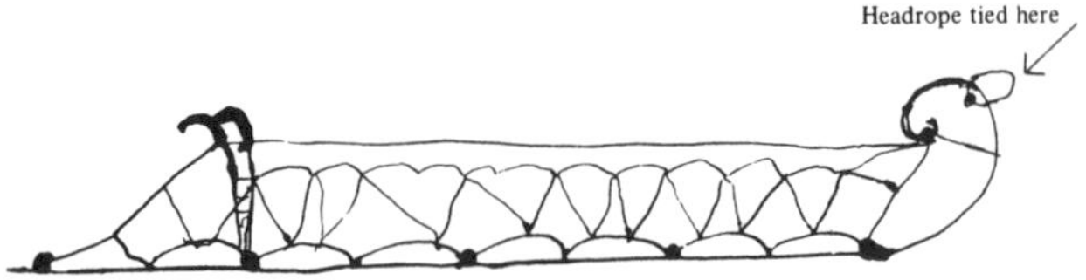

Headrope tied here

This is a two-piece sled, two boards each 8 inches wide, total width 16 inches, lashed together by means of crossbars. May be bolted. Length and width may vary.

My present sled is 7 feet long and 16 inches wide, rigged with

handlebars and cariole [le cariole]. Five dogs pull it, loaded to capacity.
The rider stands in the back end, handlebars in reach. Rider gets cold and runs behind, holding headrope [to get warmed up].
My drawings are poor.

Jan. 15, 1963,
Fort Simpson, N.W.T.

Mrs. Molson:

Your letter and money came last week and just in time. I had borrowed money to charter a plane to Sibbeston Lake and bring meat to us. I used the money to pay this bill and had food to tide us over the holidays. Lots of snow down here and cold, 47 below this morning. Jane and I both [had] the flu, but it's over now. Jane wants her teeth fixed and we'll go back when it's done.

I will write a longer letter next time. Thank you very much for the money, and I'll send you a souvenir for Easter.

Goodbye and God bless you.

Regards,
Johnny Tetso

April 18, 1963,
Fort Simpson, N.W.T.

Mr. and Mrs. Molson,

We are sending this little toboggan, which is made exactly like the one we use for winter travel in this part of the country. We will like it very much if you will accept it as a gift and souvenir of your trip north. As you were asking for drawings of toboggans, it will give you a good idea of a big one that dogs pull.

As factory-made, ready-to-use toboggans in Hudson's Bay store cost about $67, and money is not always within our reach, I make our own toboggans out of birch. This is just as good as one bought from store and has fooled some people.

Pretty soon we will be putting our toboggan away for the summer, but right now we have lots of snow and more will come later on. The coldest we had was 57 below in early February. Now the weather is really pleasant, but our spring is still about a month away. We say spring only when we see running water. This makes it a rather long winter, doesn't it? We're used to this and will take it in stride if all goes well.

We have been away from Simpson since January, with one quick trip in for groceries. The winter furs are down in prices, but the beaver price is good this year and am looking forward to a good spring hunt. Muskrats are scarce now, and I don't expect much from that angle, but beaver will be the main thing. Easter time we will be in town, and this is usually the last time that we come by dog team. Our next trip in will be by boat in June.

We have a gramophone for which we can't buy records here in Simpson, and have included a list of songs we would like to get. We are sure that you people could do us a favour in securing these records for us. Our kids love music, but what few records we have are all cracked and awful scratched by use. If you send us the records, do it in June, as we will be away till that time.

Thank you so much for your interesting letters that we have been receiving from you, and hope ours find you feeling the same way we do.

Sincerely,

Johnny Tetso and Jane

P.S. If sending records, do include the bill, as we want to pay for them. The *National Geographic* magazine has been coming since February. There was one particular story of moose vs wolf that I liked, and I agree with all the author says about wolves. I have watched them myself, from my distance, of course.

It got real good and warm before Easter till the 18th, and then north wind started to blow, all mud, snow and water froze hard, and it feels like winter again. This will last till early May, I know. Will write if in town.

Sincerely,
John Tetso

June 10th, 1963,
Ft. Simpson, N.W.T.

Dear Mrs. Molson:

We are now back in Simpson from the spring hunt, which did not turn out too good. More hunters than the hunted. And to make things worse, my kicker broke down on me. Just made enough to make both ends meet. But we are in good health and will take care of things, I guess.

May, 1963 will be long remembered. First the flu that filled the hospital with sick people, then the flood that made people run away from their own home. Our house was flooded, but the only damage was 100 lbs of dog food and lots of cleaning up.

Thanks very much for the two parcels and your willingness to help us with the records and a page in the *North* paper. I shall include a brief biography of myself as requested by the editor. I'm sorry I do not have any pictures suitable to accompany the article. Later on, I will write for them again and will send some then. I will not forget to send you some too, but I have to wait till they're developed.

The last snowfall was May the twenty-third and it snowed about a foot deep too. This was only short-lived, and right now the mosquitoes are bad at nights. The flies will [be] worse later on. People are busy planting in gardens now, and nothing has sprouted yet, no flowers.

Thanks again for your kindheartedness, and I will write a longer letter next time when I use my typewriter. Till then, good health and God bless you.

Sincerely,
Johnny Tetso

North
Editor

I am 43 years old. Three of these years were spent at the Sacred Heart School of Fort Providence, N.W.T. I have one son and two daughters. I come from a large family. My parents are still alive, though old. I have been in native politics and was Indian Chief for two years, but quit because of low pay, $25 a year. I have personally met Prince Philip on his trans-Canada tour. Been a trapper all my life and now write a few pieces about my experiences for a local paper. I have lots of bush know-how and can be hired as a guide if wanted.

signed Johnny Tetso

Aug. 8, 1963,
Willow River, N.W.T.

Mrs. J. David Molson,

Well how's the world treating you nice people out there today? We are all fine here, including the children, and hope this finds you the same. I just happened to be making a trip into town from Willow River for a few groceries and thought I'd drop a few lines.

We have [been] away from town since May, after selling our spring catch, and I'm very busy cutting telephone poles during the two months that trees can be peeled. I and four other men cut over two thousand poles, and we are getting set to skid them to the river. We also must have killed over twice as many mosquitoes doing that too.

We have received the parcels of clothes just as they were sent, and I thank you very much for them. The shirts and shoes were just fine, and I already wore out one pair of shoes walking in the bush. We gave some of these clothes away to some needy people too, telling them that the Molson people sent it. Some of us natives are not educated and seem to think that all white people are alike. I have been talking and explaining things to people like these, that there are people who regard them as fellow beings. I like doing this kind of work to help people, but sometimes it's hard when a person does not know a word of English.

I have written a story of my spring hunt and I like it very much if you good people could give it to the editors of *North*.

together with the photos. These pictures could be returned to you and you may keep them. Like you said, I felt wonderful to know that my story would be published and would like to contribute a few later on.

Thank you again for the clothes, letters, etc. I [would] certainly like to meet and talk with you fine people again and hope it comes soon. I must close now, as I have things to do, but will write again in September when we come into town.

Goodbye and our regards,

Johnny Tetso

Fort Simpson, N.W.T.
August 10, 1963.

Dear Molson;

I have just a few lines about Virginia and Flornece [sic] and me. I want to say a few lines about my holiday and the two girls. I heard that you say to draw you a picture of our own. We have draw you a picture of our own even Flornece draw one. I remember the toys you sent us for Christmas and we thank you. Flornece and Virginia are going to school. I don't know if I am going to school this year, but my father will tell if I am going to school. We are now at Willow River when my father shot moose and two ran away. They had wanted some gass from Simpson when Mr. Browing passed Willow River to go to Wrigley. He will come back after going to Wrigley to talk to my father how much tree he has cut and where he cut them. We are glad to have our holiday at Willow River again.

Your Sincerely,
Florence, Virginia and Ernest

September 16, 1963
Ft. Simpson, N.W.T.

Dear Mrs. Molson,

We are now back in Simpson and preparing for winter on the trapline. We are fine, including the children. Our two girls are back in school, too. Ernest is going with us this year, so I will have company on the line. He is just anxious and raring to go.

The price of fur has been improving for the last two years and this encourages me quite a bit. So we plan to go 100 miles and stay till past Xmas and New Year's and make enough money to buy me a power toboggan if all goes well.

If I'm lucky, I might be able to send you a silver fox if I catch one, but I have to keep my fingers crossed for that. Not many native trappers go out of town now, as the Government has built houses for them in town and they live in them year 'round. Most of my friends were good in the bush but they've changed since they moved in. I guess time is never still, but some of them are better off in the bush.

We've had a very light snowfall here just lately and the weather is turning cold all the time. I expect early freezeup, as spring came too early this year.

Next time, you will be hearing about two trappers, one green, one seasoned. Till then, we have to say goodbye for now.

Sincerely,
John Tetso

September 17th, 1963,
Fort Simpson, N.W.T.

Mr. and Mrs. Molson:

I have just opened the package of records that you sent and

was very surprised at the amount of records. Thank you very very much. It came on the boat just today.

Our children are fine and our two girls are doing good in school. Virginia in grade 5 and Florence in grade 2. Ernest has been playing hockey last winter and likes to skate. But he will be using snowshoes this winter, as he is going with us for this year only. Next year he will be in school. He is going on thirteen this coming November. He is talking about a pair of skates for Christmas. Virginia likes ballpoint pen and red is her favourite colour. Florence likes the pocket pens that you gave them when you were making the trip down Mackenzie.

The winter is colder now, but I think we will have a spell of good weather before it freezes up. The leaves are still on the trees but it's all coloured and will be falling soon. Lots of geese are going south just lately. Yes, I will try and get a fox to send if I catch one. This will be some time in February, as we plan to stay till the end of January. I have not been paid for the poles I cut for the Company. My family was with me all summer, as we cut right on the river bank. I have sent you some pictures during the summer, did you get them? Ernest is sending one now. We are getting ready to leave town tomorrow, but I shall write again if I get a chance.

Sincerely,

John Tetso

P.S. If you send a parcel for Christmas, send it to: Virginia Tetso, c/o R.C. Hostel, Ft. Simpson. Thank you.

Jan. 22nd, 1964,
Ft. Simpson, N.W.T.

Dear Mr. and Mrs. Molson,

Thanking you for the Christmas parcel, your kind letter, and wishes, and wishing you the same. Our friends tell us we've been away too long and I have lots of bush news for you. Not all good, as my dear mother passed away just lately. I guess we're not made to last forever and some day we will be unwillingly going too.

I'm having a good trapping season this year and caught twice the amount of fur I usually catch a year. I've shipped 50 pelts and bought some supplies to take back and paid my bills. Ernest is doing real good and has caught over 20 pelts outside of weasels and squirrels. I had some fun teaching him the ways of our grandfathers. At first, when I told him to make a pen for the trap, he started building a low stage, so I stepped in and showed him. Only thing now is that some traps are too big and too strong to set. A child can be caught in it and easily break a bone of the hand. First time he caught a marten in a trap set a few yards from camp, he came back running, excited, said he caught something big. Every morning he goes to see this trap and I listen for running feet. If I hear it, I know we have another pelt. It's colder now and he is not strong enough to go far away by himself. We had 53 below before Christmas, which [is] cold even for me. Lots of snow too.

I have not caught a silver fox yet, but I hope to get one. I'm sending a cross fox for now. It is dried and just the way a trapper prepares it for market. It is yours free and I plan to send a skin of different animals each year to put on your wall for the children to see. As everything is frozen in winter here, this fox was not all thawed out when I skinned it, so you'll find a tear in one of the legs.

I will have lots to talk about when we see you come down the Mackenzie. The *Catholic Voice* is not printed any more, but the stories I've been writing are collected in a book and I shall have a copy or two for you when you come. These are to sell for 50¢ each. I had a good laugh when I got my copy of the *North* and writer turns reader. We'll be leaving soon for another spell till Easter, so I'll close for now.

Goodbye to you and family and thanks again.

Sincerely,
Johnny Tetso

Fort Willow River, N.W.T.
February 1, 1964.

Dear Mrs. Molson,

We all thank you for the cloths you send us four Christmas. And I like to see your children's drawing. I am drawing you one picture to your children. My two sisters are at school. I am staying with my father to trap. I trap 4 minks, 20 martens, 1 rat, 42 squirrels, 28 weasels. My father ship them. Goodbye for now.

Yours sincerely,
Ernest Tetso

March 30th, 1964,
Fort Simpson, N.W.T.

Dear Mrs. Molson:

We are all fine and I was just delighted to hear from you and my other friends too, who took the trouble to write us. I came all the way to Simpson from Willow River by dog team, and Jane and Ernest flew in by plane. We expect to get [back] by dog team, as the plane cost money. We have a good road all the way, as the C.N.T. built one and use it to put up the telephone lines.

All fur animals are taxed and registered before crossing the territorial border. This includes even the little weasels and squirrels. I don't think it stupid to ask a direct question, as you have said. Some people do that, like the man who asked, how do you skin a frozen animal? We never skin them frozen, as this is impossible.

My clothes for the trail gear in cold weather is usually the same. The underclothes are fleece lined. Pants are the rider kind, shirt is heavy or doubled. Heavy leather jacket and a good nylon parka, which is insulated and lined. My shoes are stuffed moccasins with feet, 1 pair woolen socks and 1 pair duffel. For the hands, we use big mitts of moose hide lined with wool material. Ski cap and earmuffs complete the outfit.

Most nights of winter are spent camping out in the open and my bed is of spruce boughs laid on frozen muskeg. My bedroll is homemade eiderdown of duck feathers, with half light and half heavy sides. I use the heavy half for the top cover in real cold weather and the lighter half in milder weather.

I was told that I was born by a campfire under the stars, so camping is nothing new to me, by now anyway! Yes, Jane knows how to shoot a gun and has shot beaver, rats, rabbits, chicken and squirrels. Most native women are, anyway. Most of her time she's busy sewing and mending. In nicer weather, she puts on slacks and snowshoes to come with me. But being a woman, she has to stay home certain times, you know.

We were a bit disappointed to hear that you cancelled the Mackenzie trip for this year, but I guess time will slip by in no time. We have quite a collection of photos dating back to my school days and were planning to show them to you.

Right now I'm real busy, as the book is coming soon and I have some tape recording to do before we leave.

Thank you for the letter. Good health to you and family from us all.

Sincerely, John Tetso

P.S. You may send film if you wish to. Our camera takes 620 film. We will be back here in early June if all goes well.

June 8th, 1964,
Ft. Simpson, N.W.T.

Dear Mrs. Molson,

We are now back in Simpson after a rather cold but successful spring hunt. The children are fine and so are we. They were with us for the weekend, Virginia is the only who appears to be growing and is in the beanpole stage. Ernest is growing too, but it's hard to notice because he was home with us all winter and Virginia we have not seen for a long time. Florence thinks she is still a baby after two years at school and in grade 2.

Spring was rather delayed this year, but I had a good beaver hunt and got 40 for this year. I had Ernest and another man with me for company. We travelled by packing our hunting gear with some pack dogs and camping by little rivers, where beaver would go. Ernest has his own gun and shells, was very anxious to shoot muskrats but these were scarce. We only shot and trapped 9 altogether. Ernest shot 2 and 1 beaver. He was not bad with a gun and I'm going to get him a better one. I'll sum it all up and call it a good year for us, trapping year, that is.

I and George Boots have saved enough to have a power toboggan next winter. It's coming this summer. We might even talk to you on the phone, as we want a phone at Willow River, but we are only talking about it and the thing is not a reality yet. Willow River is good to us and we want to [stay] there again next winter if all goes fine.

My book is out now and I'm sending one. It is not so hot around Simpson, but I think it will hit good in other places and I'm busy doing that now. In other words, I'm in the struggling stage. The trouble is some of the stories had appeared and [been] read by the people around here before the publication of the book.

Thank you for the past letters, gifts, etc. We got your parcel with the films, pens, bows, just the other day and we plan to expose them and send them. You have them developed and the photos will be yours. We will keep one for winter scenes, which I'm sure you will like.

There is not much to say now, as the news is good all around, so will close now till next time. The whole family joins and wishes yours good health and our regards.

Sincerely,
John Tetso

Willow River, N.W.T.
July 17th, 1964

Dear Mrs. Molson,

Enclosed here are some photos that we have taken so far and we hope you will like them. We shall keep a roll of film for some winter shots and that will be sent later.

We are all fine and in good health and that includes the children too. We left Simpson on the 8th of this month and will be away till September 10th, or sooner. A lot depends on the weather when we travel by open boat. It is usually stormy in the first part of September too.

There was not much doing in town this year and the greater majority of the local labour force is idle. Machines are doing what we once were doing and that's hard on some people. I will be busy myself, trying to keep pace with the times. I will try and make the violin you have requested and if it's ready, I shall send it when we come back to Simpson. Also the books in time enough for your Christmas distribution. I have been getting letters from all over since the book was out and that is very nice to know some good people.

I shall write again when we come back. Thank you for thinking of us and writing.

Sincerely,
John Tetso

P.S. The CBC in Montreal will be using the text of my book on the Sunday program "On the Trail". This will be in the fall by September.

Fort Simpson, N.W.T.
Sept. 23, 1964

Dear Mrs. Molson,

I am sorry this is not John Writing the letter. This is his son, Earnest, who is writing the letter.

He died last Sunday. He was making the violin, but he did not finish it.

We came to town on Tuesday. My two sisters are going to school. But I am going to stay with my mother. Just to cut wood and cook for the dogs.

I am sorry this is all what I am going to say for now!

From Ernest Testso